A Reader's Guide to George Orwell

A Reader's Guide to George Orwell

Jeffrey Meyers

Littlefield, Adams & Company

1977

First Published in the United States of America by
LITTLEFIELD, ADAMS & CO.
81 Adams Drive, Totowa, N.J. 07512

© 1975 THAMES AND HUDSON LTD, LONDON

All rights reserved. No part of this book may be reproduced in any form without permission in writing from
the publisher except by a reviewer who wishes to quote
brief passages in connection with a review written for
inclusion in a magazine, newspaper or broadcast.

Library of Congress Cataloging in Publication Data

Meyers, Jeffrey.
    A reader's guide to George Orwell.

    (Littlefield, Adams quality paperbacks; 339)
    Bibliography: p.
    Includes index.
    1. Orwell, George, 1903-1950—Criticism and inter-
pretation.   I.   Title.
PR6029.R8Z737   1977   828'.9'1209   77–13790
ISBN 0–8226–0339–X

PRINTED IN THE UNITED STATES OF AMERICA

For
Kenneth

Chapters from this book have appeared in somewhat different form in *University Review, Philological Quarterly, Arizona Quarterly, Studies in the 20th Century, Ariel, English Miscellany* and *American Notes and Queries*.

CONTENTS

Introduction

When I look back upon resolutions of improvement and amendments, which have year after year been made and broken, either by negligence, forgetfulness, vicious idleness, casual interruption, or morbid infirmity, I find that so much of my life has stolen unprofitably away, and that I can descry by retrospection scarcely a few single days properly and vigorously employed.

Samuel Johnson, *Diary*, April 1775

There has literally been not one day in which I did not feel that I was idling, that I was behind with the current job, & that my total output was miserably small. Even at the periods when I was working 10 hours a day on a book, or turning out 4 or 5 articles a week, I have never been able to get away from this neurotic feeling.

George Orwell, *Diary*, early 1949

THESE PASSAGES ARE SIMILAR in the fervour of their unjustified self-torment, for 'no disease of the imagination is so difficult of cure, as that which is complicated with the dread of guilt'.[1] Both Johnson and Orwell had unhappy childhoods, struggled long with severe illness and bitter poverty, spent many years as hack journalists and did not achieve fame until their mid-forties. Both men were independent, combative, harsh on themselves and others, and often wrong-headed in a fascinating way. Both had limited imaginations but great critical faculties; and their satire was an expression of high principle, integrity and compassion. Both were pessimistic, patriotic, pragmatic, courageous, common-sensical, intellectually curious, scrupulously honest, fundamentally decent, oddly humorous and quintessentially English.

But their similarities go beyond personal characteristics, for Orwell's impact on the cultural life of his time is analogous to Johnson's role in his society. In his periodical writing and *reportage* Orwell's personality, like Johnson's, is closely identified with his books, and he is culturally important as the creator not only of a body of literary works but also of a particular set of values. Orwell is the last in the tradition of English moralists – Johnson, Blake, Lawrence – whose indignation and passionate intensity are almost prophetic.

As an observer of the life of the poor and a writer of political pamphlets, Orwell had important predecessors in the nineteenth century. Like Cobbett, Mayhew and Dickens, he informed a largely middle-class audience about the actual details of working-class life which he himself had observed and shared. But, unlike their work, Orwell's social and political writing involves not only the accurate depiction of poverty and oppression, but also an attempt to use his experiences to test himself and define his values. Since Orwell's narrative voice is so vital a part of his books, his created personality has great moral and political relevance. Indeed, Orwell's *persona* in *Down and Out in Paris and London*, *The Road to Wigan Pier* and *Homage to Catalonia* fulfils many of the functions of the hero in a novel: he is a person with whom we may identify, through whom we may discover, and against whom we may measure and judge.

All Orwell's books are autobiographical and spring from his psychological need to work out the pattern and meaning of his personal experience; his great triumph is his ability to transform his early guilt and awareness of what it means to be a victim, described in 'Such, Such Were the Joys', into a compassionate ethic of responsibility, a compulsive sharing in the suffering and degradation of others. The analysis of *Burmese Days* and 'Shooting an Elephant' shows how Orwell experienced and then tried to understand the role of the oppressor. The guilt about his imperialistic role, expressed in both these works, suggests his similarity to French writers like Malraux and Sartre, who saw themselves 'responsible in the face of history' for moral awareness and social justice, and whose ethic of responsibility goes beyond the traditional claims for artistic integrity and personal commitment, and both limits and liberates their artistic powers.

In his essay on Yeats, Orwell notes that the best writers of our time – Yeats, Eliot, Pound, Joyce – have been reactionary in tendency, and he deliberately opposed this tradition and tried to awaken public opinion during the years of Fascist aggression. Like Solzhenitsyn, Orwell was the conscience of his age, and his whole life was a struggle against barbarism and for what he called 'comparative decency': a sane, clean, friendly world, without fear and without injustice. But on the rare occasions when he portrays this decent world – George Bowling's childhood in *Coming Up For Air*, and Animal Farm just after the revolution – it is inevitably destroyed by corruption, brutality and war.

Orwell opened himself to the suffering of others and felt it was his vocation to warn men about the future. Despite Orwell's radical pessimism, E. M. Forster writes that he 'tried to ameliorate a world which is bound to be unhappy. A true liberal, he hoped to help through small things.'[2] An extended simile from Orwell's review of Muggeridge's *The Thirties* combines a commonplace cruelty with a fine perception to produce a far-fetched yet convincing symbol of the human condition:

> I thought of a rather cruel trick I once played on a wasp. He was sucking jam on my plate, and I cut him in half. He paid no attention, merely went on with his meal, while a tiny stream of jam trickled out of his severed oesophagus. Only when he tried to fly away did he grasp the dreadful thing that had happened to him. It is the same with modern man. The thing that has been cut away is his soul, and there was a period – twenty years, perhaps – during which he did not notice it.[3]

Through his moral commitment and exemplary honesty, Orwell wanted to draw attention to man's lost soul and then attempt to restore it.

Orwell's mind has a uniquely curious, lively, random and miscellaneous quality and, in its lack of formal training, seems to resemble his own description of Charles Reade: 'a man of what one

might call penny-encyclopaedic learning. He possessed vast stocks
of disconnected information with a lively narrative gift' (II.34).
And Orwell's comment on Bertrand Russell is also self-reflective:
'He has rather an eclectic mind, he is capable of saying shallow things
and profoundly interesting things in alternate sentences. . . . But he
has an essentially *decent* intellect, a kind of intellectual chivalry which
is far rarer than mere cleverness' (I.376). Orwell was harsh but fair
with his intellectual opponents, and when he realized he had been
unjust he was chivalrous enough to apologize publicly. In 'Inside the
Whale', for example, he wrote that some years previously, in *The
Road to Wigan Pier*, 'I described Auden as "a sort of gutless Kipling".
As criticism this was quite unworthy, indeed it was merely a spiteful
remark' (I.511).

Orwell's finest characteristics are a Conradian concern with the
isolation in which human beings live and with their intense longing
for compassion and solidarity; a generosity of spirit that extends to
enemy prisoners, French collaborators and Fascist war criminals;
intellectual honesty; clear and balanced judgment; and the courage
to speak out against any mean or cowardly attitude, and to defend
dangerous and unpopular views. As he says, 'To write in plain,
vigorous language one has to think fearlessly, and if one thinks
fearlessly one cannot be politically orthodox' (IV.66). Though
Orwell was a socialist, he never adhered to a party line and always
criticized the Left as freely as he did the Right. He combined commitment with righteousness, and his political motive was 'to push
the world in a certain direction, to alter other people's idea of the
kind of society they should strive after. . . . What I have most
wanted to do throughout the past ten years', he wrote in 1946, 'is
to make political writing into an art. My starting point is always a
feeling of partisanship, a sense of injustice' (I.4,6).

Like D. H. Lawrence, who says, 'I write because I want folk – English folk – to alter, and have more sense,'[4] Orwell was a rebel and a
prophet intensely dissatisfied with the decaying spirit of England
and the sharp decline of European civilization. Lawrence turned
inward and treated the problem and the cure in an extremely

personal way: he wanted to make a new world by radically changing the feelings of men and women. Orwell tried to find social
solutions to the crisis of civilization felt within the individual: he
attempted to make himself and others aware of their responsibility
and their capacity to deal with political problems.

Orwell writes of Lawrence that

> like Dickens, he is a 'change of heart' man and constantly insisting that
> life here and now would be all right if only you looked at it a little
> differently. But what he is demanding is a movement away from our
> mechanised civilisation, which is not going to happen, and which he
> knows is not going to happen. Therefore his exasperation with the
> present turns once more into an idealisation of the past. . . .
> The ultimate subject-matter of nearly all Lawrence's books is the failure
> of contemporary men, especially in the English-speaking countries, to
> live their lives intensely enough. . . . Granted that they can be fully alive,
> he doesn't much care what social or political or economic system they
> live under. (1.507, 11.202)

A dissatisfaction with the modern age led Orwell to idealize the
recent past of his childhood just as Lawrence idealized the distant
past of his race. But Orwell, unlike Lawrence, was extremely concerned about what social system he lived under.

Orwell's books deal with two dominant themes – poverty and
politics – or, as he put it, 'the twin nightmares that beset nearly
every modern man, the nightmare of unemployment and the nightmare of State interference' (IV.247). The autobiographical *Down and
Out in Paris and London* (1933), the novels *A Clergyman's Daughter*
(1935) and *Keep the Aspidistra Flying* (1936), and the *reportage The
Road to Wigan Pier* (1937) deal with the first theme; *Burmese Days*
(1934), *Homage to Catalonia* (1938), *Animal Farm* (1945) and *1984*
(1949) with the second; while *Coming Up For Air* (1939), an apocalyptic novel that records the vision of a world destroyed, is a transitional work that precedes the major wartime essays and concerns an
unsuccessful attempt to escape from both nightmares. There is a
continuity, consistency (and repetition) of Orwell's major ideas;
and a unity, pattern and development in all his books, which are
closely related to each other and to the essays.

In the struggle to alert his audience to social and political injustice, Orwell's weapon was language, and he emphasizes the value of the pamphlet as an art form: 'the pamphlet ought to be *the* literary form of an age like our own. We live in a time when political passions run high, channels of free expression are dwindling, and organised lying exists on a scale never before known. For plugging the holes in history the pamphlet is the ideal form' (II.285). Orwell's reports from Spain during the Civil War are the best example of how he attempted, almost single-handedly, to provide the factual basis of history. Polemical pamphleteering played an important part in Orwell's political books, for *Homage to Catalonia* contains long sections of political analysis, the Appendix on Newspeak in *1984* is a self-contained pamphlet, and he considered bringing out *Animal Farm* as a two-shilling pamphlet when he was unable to publish it as a book during the war. The qualities that Orwell characteristically associates with good prose are honesty and directness, and his concept of the pamphlet is not the scurrilous broadside aimed at settling a score, but a communication of truth. As John Wain says, 'The virtues which the polemic kind demands – urgency, incisiveness, clarity and humour – he possessed in exactly the right combination.'[5]

Orwell is the great master of colloquial ease, and believes that 'concrete words are better than abstract ones, and that the shortest way of saying anything is always the best' (III.26). His vivid and direct, flexible and far-ranging style is always readable and interesting, and moves from witty aphorisms:

> Poetry on the air sounds like the Muses in striped trousers (II.334)

to a strange Swiftian presentation of the seemingly familiar:

> All our food springs ultimately from dung and dead bodies, the two things which of all others seem to us the most horrible (IV.222)

and the startling, almost Donne-like opening of 'England Your England':

> As I write, highly civilised human beings are flying overhead, trying to kill me (II.56).

In a typical passage from 'The Rediscovery of Europe', Orwell relates:

> When I was a small boy and was taught history ... you were given to understand that what came afterwards was completely different from what had gone before. It was almost like a clock striking. For instance, in 1499 you were still in the Middle Ages, with knights in plate armour riding at one another with long lances, and then suddenly the clock struck 1500, and you were in something called the Renaissance, and everyone wore ruffs and doublets and was busy robbing treasure ships on the Spanish Main. (II.197)

In this humorous exaggeration, Orwell conveys the simplistic mentality of his teacher by effective use of a simile and a series of historical clichés that suggest knights hurrying to change their costume in time for the next age. It is worth noticing (as Orwell would say) that three of his novels begin with a reference to time. *A Clergyman's Daughter* starts with the ringing of an alarm clock; *Keep the Aspidistra Flying* opens rather prosaically with 'The clock struck half past two'; but the first sentence of *1984*, 'It was a bright cold day in April, and the clocks were striking thirteen,' conveys the uneasy menace of a military régime.

Orwell's ideas about style are similar to those of Samuel Butler, whom he read in prep school and named as one of 'the writers I care most about and never grow tired of' (II.24). Butler writes in his *Notebooks* of the beauty of simplicity:

> A man may, and ought to, take a great deal of pains to write clearly, tersely and euphemistically: he will write many a sentence three or four times over – to do more than this is worse than not rewriting at all: he will be at great pains to see that he does not repeat himself, to arrange his matter in a way that shall best enable the reader to master it, to cut out superfluous words and, even more, eschew irrelevant matter: but in each case he will be thinking not of his own style but of his reader's convenience.[6]

And Orwell also emphasizes the importance of stylistic care, clarity and precision in his Notebooks and in 'Politics and the English Language':

Virtually all that I wrote was written at least twice, and my books as a whole three times – individual passages as many as five or ten times. (II.350)

A scrupulous writer, in every sentence that he writes, will ask himself at least four questions, thus: What am I trying to say? What words will express it? What image or idiom will make it clearer? Is this image fresh enough to have an effect? And he will probably ask himself two more: Could I put it more shortly? Have I said anything that is avoidably ugly? (IV.135)

And Butler's aphorism, 'A man's style in any art should be like his dress – it should attract as little attention as possible,'[7] is very close to Orwell's belief that 'one can write nothing readable unless one constantly struggles to efface one's personality. Good prose is like a window pane' (I.7).

It is essential, however, to distinguish between Orwell's professed intention and the actual effect of his prose. When he records in his Diary for The Road to Wigan Pier, 'A few rats running slowly through the snow, presumably weak with hunger' (I.177), the image produces a complex conjunction of pity and abhorrence in the reader and achieves a strong emotional effect by the apparent excision of emotion from the language. The surviving rats run slowly because they are starving and their tameness, an attractive quality in wild animals, is horrible here because it brings the weak though frightening rats uncomfortably out in the open. In an environment where even the most intense scavengers go hungry, the rats suggest filthy, hungry, predatory *people* (the fresh image has an effect), the oppressed poor whose desperate situation preys on the conscience of Orwell's audience, whom he has edged into interested sympathy. Orwell developed a forceful and persuasive prose style by skilfully arranging facts, and the attempt to efface his personality paradoxically produces a distinctive style and recognizable *persona*.

This technique is frequently employed by Swift, who satirizes his own *personae*. But Orwell, who often ridicules himself and points out his own mistakes and misconceptions, always identifies with his *persona*. His most sophisticated use of this *persona* is in Homage to

Catalonia, a war memoir related to the novels about the Great War narrated from the victim's viewpoint, in which Orwell combines personal narrative with factual reporting, and creates a unique form by uniting two different kinds of 'truth'.

These literary gifts are important for a novelist, yet Orwell's early novels, which establish the circular pattern where the characters attempt to escape from their habitual lives and are forced back into them, are ultimately unsatisfactory. In these early novels and social documentaries, his need to verify ideas by personal experience and objective observation – his compulsion to be honest – produces an effective novelistic projection of the self in the *reportage*, but inhibits the creation of an imaginative world. For he could not create characters *outside* himself and is not successful in grafting social analysis and political purpose on to the form of the traditional novel.

The analysis of *Animal Farm* and *1984*, however, shows how this kind of artful literalness could be extremely successful once Orwell discovered the appropriate form of expression. *Animal Farm*, influenced by Swift, combines the elements not only of the pamphlet and the novel, but also of fantasy, fable, satire and allegory, to produce a convincing warning of the Soviet betrayal of revolutionary principles. *1984*, an anti-utopian satire influenced by Swift, Dostoyevsky, Zamyatin and Trotsky, is a synthesis and culmination of all Orwell's previous books that returns to the themes of childhood vulnerability and guilt expressed in 'Such, Such Were the Joys' and transmutes them into a powerful political myth.

Orwell engages himself with political reality through the union of conscience and commitment; he enlarges our sense of the social and political entity that surrounds us. This book reveals how Orwell's works and ideas evolved from his personal experience and masochistic guilt, but it also considers the *kind* of literature produced by a sensitive and committed artist. It shows that Orwell's honesty and political purpose influenced his literary experiments in several *genres*, and suggests that his creation of a new kind of personal narrative, which has become a distinctive contemporary form, made him the greatest modern essayist and reporter.

1 The Autobiographical Strain

> Such, such were the joys
> When we all, girls and boys,
> In our youth time were seen
> On the Echoing Green.
> WILLIAM BLAKE, 'The Echoing Green'

I

ORWELL'S WORKS are closely connected to the events of his life. He did not have great powers of imagination and could write only about things he had actually observed, so he deliberately sought out material he could write about and used every scrap of experience in his books. Orwell found his way slowly and arrived late. He was an Etonian, colonial policeman, tramp, dishwasher, hop-picker, tutor, teacher, reviewer and pseudo-Georgian poet before he published his first book at the age of thirty. And during the next fifteen years he was a book dealer, soldier, farmer, film critic, broadcaster, editor, war correspondent and, all too frequently, hospital patient, as well as an author.

Orwell was always extremely reticent about his personal affairs and emotions, so we know little about how his moral and intellectual character was formed in his earliest years. Both sides of his family had been connected with the East. His paternal grandfather was an Anglican priest in Australia and India; and his maternal grandfather, who was French, was a teak merchant in Moulmein, Burma. His father, Richard Blair, was a sub-deputy agent in the Opium Department of the Indian Civil Service, which supervised the legalized opium trade with China. Orwell's family was part of that 'upper-middle class, which had its heyday in the eighties and nineties, with Kipling as its poet laureate, and was a sort of mound of wreckage left behind when the tide of Victorian prosperity receded'.[1]

Orwell – whose real name was Eric Arthur Blair – was the second of three children. He was born in 1903 in Motihari, Bengal, situated on the bank of a lake in the state of Bihar, between Patna and Katmandu. Like Thackeray, Kipling and Durrell, he spent his first years in India before he was sent to England at the age of four to begin school. Kipling's *Something of Myself* (1937) gives a lyrical description of a secure Indian childhood, protected by the gentleness and affection of bearer and *ayah*; and Fraser writes of Durrell that 'The Indian childhood, the heat, the colour, the Kiplingesque social atmosphere, deeply affected his childish imagination.'[2] Both Thackeray and Kipling stress the wrenching trauma of leaving India at the age of five. In *The Newcomes* (1853), Thackeray writes, 'What a strange pathos seems to me to accompany all our Indian story! ... The family must be broken up. . . . In America it is from the breast of a poor slave that a child is taken; in India it is from the wife.'[3] Kipling's 'Baa Baa Black Sheep', which Orwell considered one of the best short stories in English, describes his sudden departure from servants and parents ('through no fault of their own, they had lost all their world'), and the horrors of an alien family that engulfs him with meanness and cruelty. Like Orwell, Kipling endured inexplicable accusations of crimes, constant fear of punishment, unjust beatings, terrifying threats of hell and utter despair, and he concludes that 'when young lips have drunk deep of the bitter waters of Hate, Suspicion, and Despair, all the Love in the world will not wholly take away that knowledge'.[4] Unlike the accounts of Thackeray and Kipling, Orwell's description of childhood, though entirely subjective, has no self-pity or false pathos.

Orwell attended the local primary school at Henley-on-Thames, and lived in the strange atmosphere that Anglo-Indian families recreated in order to protect themselves from the realities of life in

England. George Bowling, the hero of *Coming Up For Air*, married into one of these families, describes it with familiar disdain and compares the exotic but self-deceptive microcosm to a diseased growth:

> As soon as you set foot inside the front door you're in India in the eighties. You know the kind of atmosphere. The carved teak furniture, the brass trays, the dusty tiger-skulls on the wall, the Trichinopoly cigars, the red-hot pickles, the yellow photographs of chaps in sun-helmets, the Hindustani words that you're expected to know the meaning of, the everlasting anecdotes of the tiger-shoots and what Smith said to Jones in Poona in '87. It's a sort of little world of their own that they've created, like a kind of cyst.[5]

Orwell writes in 'Such, Such Were the Joys' (1947), which depicts the loss of innocence during the agonizing years of adolescence, that even while at home his early childhood was not altogether happy. Orwell's father, who was fifty when he sent his family to England in 1907, spent the next four years in India and did not return home until 1912, the year after Orwell went away to preparatory school. 'One ought to love one's father,' Orwell observes, 'but I know very well that I merely disliked my father, whom I had barely seen before I was eight and who appeared to me simply as a gruff-voiced elderly gentleman forever saying "Don't".'[6]

Sir Steven Runciman describes Mrs Blair, who had grown up in Burma and was eighteen years younger than her husband, as 'a charming woman, a bit exotic and gypsy-looking, with her bright-coloured scarves and gold hoop ear-rings'.[7] But Orwell, who always found it extremely difficult to express his deepest feelings, admits that as a child, 'I never felt love for any mature person, except my mother, and even her I did not trust. . . . Not to expose your true feelings to an adult seems to me to be instinctive from the age of seven or eight onwards,' that is, from the time he went to preparatory school. Orwell later startled a contemporary at Eton by cynically criticizing his parents: 'He'd been the first person I had ever heard running down his own father and mother.'[8]

An archetypal image of a warm and secure lower-class family hearth, which Orwell never had and always wanted, appears again and again in his works as an idealized domestic portrait that contrasts with the artificial ambiance of his own home and reflects his sense of deprivation:

> In a working-class home . . . you breathe a warm, decent, deeply human atmosphere which is not so easy to find elsewhere. . . . On winter evenings after tea, when the fire glows in the open range and dances mirrored in the steel fender, Father, in shirt-sleeves, sits in the rocking-chair at one side of the fire reading the racing finals, while Mother sits on the other with her sewing.[9]

But the positively-presented adults of Dickens's working-class families, like Clara Peggotty and Joe Gargery, cannot be found in Orwell's books. Though he allows himself to postulate the idealized existence of such families, his closer examination of lower-class life, from *Down and Out in Paris and London* to *1984*, portrays the daily deprivation and boredom rather than the favourable aspects of this life.

Orwell states that at eight years old he was suddenly separated from his family and, like Dorothy Hare[10] and Winston Smith, 'flung into a world of force and fraud and secrecy, like a gold-fish into a tank full of pike'; and the echo of Milton's Satan ('by fraud or guile/What force effected not') emphasizes the hellish aspect of St Cyprian's school in Eastbourne. Like Gordon Comstock in *Keep the Aspidistra Flying*, Orwell won a scholarship to a mediocre preparatory school where he spent the crucial years from eight to fourteen. He confesses that he was miserable and 'lonely, and soon developed disagreeable mannerisms which made me unpopular throughout my schooldays' (1.1).

St Cyprian's intended to exploit his intelligence, and his family, who made financial sacrifices for his education, counted on him to succeed and retrieve their diminishing fortunes. He states that one of the school codes was 'an almost neurotic dread of poverty, and, above all, the assumption . . . that money and privilege are the things that matter'. When Orwell boastfully adds a few hundred pounds to his father's income, a Russian boy then calculates that *his* father has more than two hundred times as much money. In school Orwell felt guilty because he did not have money, and also because he wanted to have it.

In his essay on Dali, Orwell states with profound pessimism, 'Autobiography is only to be trusted when it reveals something disgraceful. A man who gives a good account of himself is probably lying, since any life when viewed from the inside is simply a series of defeats' (III.156).[11] Orwell's feelings about St Cyprian's, which he anatomized and condemned in 'Such, Such Were the Joys', were so intense, his revelations so painful, that the essay was not published during his lifetime.

Cyril Connolly, who went up to Eton with Orwell and remained his lifelong friend, gives a different and rather more pleasant picture of their preparatory school in *Enemies of Promise*. 'I was a stage rebel,' writes Connolly, 'Orwell was a true one. Tall, pale, with his flaccid cheeks, and matter-of-fact, supercilious voice, he was one of those boys who seem born old. . . . The remarkable thing about Orwell was that he alone among the boys was an intellectual, and not a parrot, for he thought for himself, read Shaw and Samuel Butler, and rejected not only St Wulfric's [St Cyprian's], but the war, the Empire, Kipling, Sussex and Character.'[12] Even at school Orwell had a passion for prophecy, and he authoritatively told Connolly, 'Whoever wins this war, we shall emerge a second-rate nation.'[13] Orwell's contribution to the war effort was two patriotic poems, 'Kitchener' (on the death by water of the Minister of War), and 'Awake! Young Men of England', which was published in the local Oxfordshire newspaper:

> Oh! give me the strength of a lion,
>   The wisdom of Reynard the Fox,
> And then I'll hurl troops at the Germans,
>   And give them the hardest of knocks.[14]

When Connolly's book was published in 1938, Orwell said to him, 'I wonder how you can write abt St Cyprian's. It's all like an awful nightmare to me' (I.343).

Orwell's reaction to this nightmare, a self-destructive expression of protest and fear, is recorded in his startling opening sentence:

'Soon after I arrived at St Cyprian's . . . I began wetting my bed.'
The result of this shameful practice was two beatings which caused
that deeper grief which is peculiar to childhood: 'a sense of desolate
loneliness and helplessness, of being locked up not only in a hostile
world but in a world of good and evil where the rules were such that
it was actually not possible for me to keep them. . . . I had a conviction of sin and folly and weakness, such as I do not remember to have
felt before. . . . This acceptance of guilt lay unnoticed in my memory
for twenty or thirty years,' that is, during the whole course of his
life, from schooldays until he tried to purge this guilt by writing the
essay in the 1940s.

The bed-wetting was only the first of endless episodes that made
Orwell feel guilty: he was poor, he was lazy and a failure, un-
grateful and unhealthy, disgusting and dirty-minded, 'weak, ugly,
cowardly, smelly'. Flip and Sambo beat and humiliated him throughout the six years, and Orwell developed the 'profound conviction
that I was no good, that I was wasting my time, wrecking my
talents, behaving with monstrous folly and wickedness and ingratitude – and all this, it seemed, was inescapable'. After a sexual scandal,
'Guilt seemed to hang in the air like a pall of smoke. . . . Till then I
had hoped that I was innocent, and the conviction of sin which now
took possession of me was perhaps all the stronger because I did not
know what I had done.'

These disturbing passages suggest the confusion and anxiety, the
guilt and absurdity, of a Kafkaesque world in which the child – who
is credulous, weak and vulnerable – is the ready and constant victim.
For he lacks any sense of proportion or probability, and is forced to
live with the anxious 'dread of offending against mysterious, terrible
laws'. The most poignant moments in 'Such, Such' come from
Orwell's realization of his own disloyalty, mendacity and hypo-
crisy, and a major theme in the essay is his retrospective horror at the
kind of person he was. He seems to be saying, 'Look what they
made me into. I was a foul little coward – but I was goaded by
deprivation, insecurity and lack of love.' Orwell may have been a
horrid though pitiful and confused child, but the school authorities,

who knew precisely what they were doing to the children, were far worse.

The themes of authority, guilt, cruelty, helplessness, isolation and misery are portrayed in the school chapter of *A Portrait of the Artist as a Young Man* (1916), which probably influenced 'Such, Such'. Both Stephen Dedalus and Orwell are bullied by the older, stronger boys: Stephen is pushed into the cold slimy water, and Orwell fears 'the daily nightmare of football – the cold, the mud . . . the gouging knees and trampling boots of the bigger boys. . . . That was the pattern of school life – a continuous triumph of the strong over the weak.' The innocent Stephen is abused and beaten by Father Dolan:

> 'Lazy idle little loafer!' cried the prefect of studies. 'Broke my glasses! An old schoolboy trick! Out with your hand this moment!'[15]

just as Orwell is by Sambo:

> 'Go on you little slacker! Go on, you idle, worthless little boy! The whole trouble with you is that you're bone and horn idle.'

And Orwell, like Joyce, is threatened with damnation and terrified by fiery sermons: 'Up to the age of about fourteen I officially believed in [Hell]. Almost certainly Hell existed, and there were occasions when a vivid sermon could scare you into fits.'

The horrors that Orwell suffered represent an archetypal childhood trauma, and the literary analogues in Dickens illuminate his situation. Orwell writes that Dickens 'had grown up near enough to poverty to be terrified of it' (1.434), and he must have recognized certain similarities between Dickens's life and his own, for they both came from a middle-class family going into decline. Orwell's cruel treatment at school was the emotional equivalent of Dickens's servitude in the blacking factory (which occurred at the same age), and both men bore scars of early poverty throughout their lives. Dickens 'prayed when I went to bed at night to be lifted out of the humiliation and neglect in which I was. I never had suffered so much before';[16] and Orwell writes of 'suffering horrors which he cannot or will not reveal'. In *Something of Myself*, Kipling explains why children never tell their family about cruel treatment at school:

Children tell little more than animals, for what comes to them they accept as eternally established. Also, badly-treated children have a clear notion of what they are likely to get if they betray the secrets of a prison-house before they are clear of it.[17]

Like Dickens, Orwell was 'on the side of the underdog, always and everywhere' (1.458), and his sympathy for the oppressed was related to his unhappy childhood.

Orwell compares St Cyprian's to Dotheboys Hall in *Nicholas Nickleby* (1839), and that infamous school, where 'lasting agonies and disfigurements are inflicted upon children by the treatment of the master',[18] influenced Orwell's portrayal of his school as a reactionary and barbaric Victorian institution. Mrs Squeers feeds the boys brimstone and treacle 'because it spoils their appetites and comes cheaper than breakfast and dinner',[19] and Orwell writes that 'Only a generation earlier it had been common for school dinners to start off with a slab of unsweetened suet pudding, which, it was frankly said, "broke the boys' appetites".' Mrs Squeers taps the crown of the boys' heads with a wooden spoon just as Sambo 'taps away at one's skull with a silver pencil'. And the scene where Squeers flogs the helpless boy who has warts on his hands and who has failed to pay his full fees is psychologically similar to Orwell's caning for bed-wetting, since both boys must confess to an imaginary crime while suffering unjust punishment.

Dickens's description of disreputable schools, Orwell's unhappy years at St Cyprian's ('The school still had a faint suggestion of the Victorian "private academy" with its "parlour boarders" '), and his teaching experience at several seedy schools from April 1932 until December 1933 when, like Lawrence, he retired early from the profession because of bad health, all contribute to his portrayal of Ringwood Academy, where Dorothy Hare teaches in *A Clergyman's Daughter*. This school chapter is Orwell's first attempt to deal with his years at St Cyprian's and, though much less successful than 'Such, Such', it is the most intense and convincing part of the novel.

Orwell alludes to the schools portrayed in the early chapters of *Nicholas Nickleby* and *David Copperfield* (1850) when he writes that

Dorothy's school is 'reminiscent of those dreary little private schools that you read about in Victorian novels'.[20] Do-the-boys Hall, St Cyprian's and Ringwood (ringworm) Academy are all more interested in money than in education:

> Both Mr. and Mrs. Squeers . . . held and considered that their business and profession was to get as much from every boy as could by possibility be screwed out of him.[21]

> It was the poor but 'clever' boys who suffered. Our brains were a gold-mine in which he had sunk money, and the dividends must be squeezed out of us. (IV.339)

> 'It's the fees I'm after, not *developing the children's minds*.'[22]

Though Orwell takes Mrs Creevy's name from *Nicholas Nickleby* (Miss La Creevy is a kind old miniature painter), she is a vicious modern version of the cruel and tyrannical Mr Creakle, master of David Copperfield's school. (When Mrs Creevy tries to smile, her face '*creaked* with the effort'.) Steerforth says Creakle is 'more ignorant than the lowest boy in the school',[23] and Mrs Creevy 'had never read a book right through in her life, and was proud of it'.[24] Creakle's assistants were both supposed to be wretchedly paid; and 'when there was hot and cold meat for dinner at Mr Creakle's table, Mr Sharp was always expected to say he preferred cold',[25] just as Dorothy is never allowed to have marmalade at breakfast. Two of the other teachers at Ringwood are like Dickensian caricatures: the drunkard Miss Strong and the weak, pathetic chemistry 'lecturer', Mr Booth. (Oddly enough, Mr Creakle, like Dorothy, 'had taken to the schooling business after being bankrupt in hops'.[26])

The atmosphere of 'Such, Such' also appears in *A Clergyman's Daughter*, for in both schools students are classified by their economic status. At Orwell's school:

> The boys of the scholarship class were not all treated alike. If the boy was the son of rich parents to whom the saving of fees was not all-important, Sambo would goad him along in a comparatively fatherly way, with jokes and digs in the ribs and perhaps an occasional tap with

the pencil, but no hair-pulling and no caning. . . . In effect there were three castes in the school.

These three castes also exist at Ringwood: the good payers are never smacked, the medium payers have their ears twisted, and the bad payers suffer unlimited abuse. Orwell states in his essay, 'I doubt whether classical education ever has been or can be successfully carried on without corporal punishment,' and at Ringwood Dorothy is forced to hit the children, 'an unforgivable thing . . . but nearly all teachers come to it in the end'.[27] The utter loneliness, the 'filthy food, the cold and lack of baths' are similar at both schools; and both Flip and Sambo and Mrs Creevy hypocritically attack Orwell and Dorothy with a stream of mean, cruel reprimand. Flip threatens:

'And do you think it's quite fair to *us*, the way you're behaving? After all we've done for you? . . . We don't *want* to have to send you away, you know, but we can't keep a boy here just to eat up our food.'

And Mrs Creevy accuses Dorothy in front of the ignorant parents of

monstrous treachery and ingratitude. . . . Phrases like 'girl that I've taken into my house', 'eating my bread' and even 'living on my charity', recurred over and over again.[28]

'Such, Such', Orwell's most poignant and, after *Animal Farm*, his most perfect work, is of the greatest value for an understanding of his character, life and books, for Orwell's self-portrayal as a vulnerable child-victim is the autobiographical archetype for his fictional anti-heroes. Just as *1984* is a final synthesis of all Orwell's major themes, so 'Such, Such', which was written at the same time, reveals the genesis and impetus of these ideas. Its central themes – poverty, fear, guilt, masochism and sickness – are developed in all his books and manifested in the pattern of his life.

Orwell's experiences in *Down and Out* are his direct reaction against, and refutation of, this privileged school ethos, just as his use of a pseudonym (George is the patron saint of England, Orwell an East Anglian river) beginning with that book is an attempt to abandon that hateful part of his life that he associated with St

Cyprian's. He writes that 'People always grow up like their names
It took me nearly thirty years to work off the effects of being called
Eric' (II.22); and when he gave up the family name of Blair, he
rejected the Scottish birth of both parents and the odious cult of
Scotland that pervaded his snobbish school. The hero of *Keep the
Aspidistra Flying* admits that ' "Gordon Comstock" was a pretty
bloody name, but then Gordon came of a pretty bloody family.
The "Gordon" part of it was Scotch, of course.'[29] Comstock's
experience at a school where nearly all the boys were richer than
himself and tormented him because of it led to his renunciation of
ambition and the world of money. As Comstock says, 'Probably the
greatest cruelty one can inflict on a child is to send it to a school
among children richer than itself. A child conscious of poverty will
suffer snobbish agonies such as a grown-up person can scarcely even
imagine.'[30] This may not be the 'greatest' cruelty, but it is the one
Orwell suffered.

Orwell's other books also reflect his childhood experiences. The
facial deformity of Flory in *Burmese Days* is the symbolic equivalent
of Orwell's feeling that he was an ugly failure, and Flory also suffers
agonies of humiliation at school. The overwhelming doom that
threatens the young Orwell also threatens Bowling in *Coming Up
For Air*; and the fearful oppression by one's fellows recurs in *Animal
Farm*. The lonely Orwell's desperate need for human comradeship
and solidarity is at the emotional core of *Homage to Catalonia*; and a
deep sympathy for the oppressed sent Orwell to Spain and put him
on the road to Wigan Pier. At St Cyprian's he learned that 'The
good and the possible never seemed to coincide,' and, in an important sense, his whole life was an attempt to bring them together.
Oppression and humiliation formed the dominant pattern of his
personal life at the time when Europe was being dominated by
Communism and Fascism.

The vivid memories of his schooldays 'always haunted' Orwell
and 'Such, Such', more an exorcism than a narrative, demonstrates
Lawrence's belief that 'One sheds one's sicknesses in books – repeats
and presents again one's emotions, to be master of them.'[31] In the

last paragraph, Orwell writes with ironic satisfaction, 'Now however, the place is out of my system for good'; but his relief was premature, for the horrors of St Cyprian's reappear with even greater force in *1984*.

More than any other novel, *1984* expresses the frightful, almost infantile vulnerability of human beings who have experienced atomic and saturation bombing, and concentration camps, which Orwell may have seen and had certainly heard of when reporting from Germany in 1945. In his study of those camps, Bruno Bettelheim, who was a prisoner in Dachau and Buchenwald, has revealed the psychological connection between regression to childhood fear and obedience, and the atmosphere of cruelty and punishment that Orwell portrays in *1984*. Bettelheim's analysis illuminates Winston's strange defensive attachment to O'Brien:

> Prisoners were particularly sensitive to being treated the way a harsh parent might act toward a helpless child. . . . Like the child who identifies with the parent, this identification helped prisoners to know intuitively what the SS expected of them. . . . Increased masochistic, passive-dependent, and childlike attitudes were 'safe' because they kept the prisoner out of conflict with the SS. But as a psychological mechanism inside the prisoner it coincided with the SS efforts to produce childlike inadequacy and dependency.[32]

Another of Bettelheim's insights concerns the relation between authority, starvation and infantilism in the concentration camps. This insight clarifies Orwell's ambivalent hunger and revulsion from food at school as well as Winston's revulsion when he looks in the mirror and sees himself as a starved skeleton:

> The infant fears his parents' displeasure lest they withhold what he needs for his very existence; for the infant, this is symbolized by food. . . . The SS reactivated this same basic fear by starving prisoners to such a degree that they lived in continuous anxiety about what food, and how much, they would get.[33]

The essential point here is that, for Orwell, the punishment and hunger that were associated with concentration camps and portrayed in the torture scenes of the novel were rooted in the terrible memories of his childhood that had never stopped haunting him.

Anthony West, in a review of Orwell's fiction, was the first to notice that 'Most of these [terrors], in *Nineteen Eighty-Four*, are of an infantile character, and they clearly derive from the experience described in *Such, Such Were the Joys* . . . . What he did in *Nineteen Eighty-Four* was to send everybody in England to an enormous Crossgates [St Cyprian's] to be as miserable as he had been.'[34] But West does not reveal how extensive the atmosphere of the prep school is in *1984*.

It is not merely that Winston was conditioned 'by games and cold water' at school and is forced to do violent physical jerks as an adult, that he works in a cubicle and in prison sits very still with his hands crossed on his knees, that during the interrogation O'Brien is both 'schoolmasterish' and 'didactic'; for many ideas in 'Such, Such' are repeated in the novel.

In school, Orwell disdained 'the hoo-ha about fresh air and cold water and keeping in hard training', and Winston dislikes Julia 'because of the atmosphere of hockey-fields and cold baths and community hikes and general clean-mindedness which she managed to carry about with her'.[35] The atmosphere of St Cyprian's, like that of Oceania, is filthy, decrepit and degrading in a mean sort of way:

> It is not easy for me to think of my schooldays without seeming to breathe in a whiff of something cold and evil-smelling – a sort of compound of sweaty stockings, dirty towels, faecal smells blowing along corridors, forks with old food between the prongs, neck-of-mutton stew, and the banging doors of the lavatories.

The imagined spies of the all-powerful Headmaster – 'it was natural that his agents should be everywhere' – are transformed into the Thought Police. The spy-trained children betray their parents in the same sneaking way that Orwell did at school: 'I accepted the codes that I found in being. Once, towards the end of my time, I even sneaked to Brown about a suspected case of homosexuality.'

Winston's ugliness, disgust and self-hatred, even before he is tortured, are very like young Orwell's: 'I had no money, I was weak, I was ugly, I was unpopular, I had a chronic cough, I was cowardly, I smelt.' Winston's inherent guilt and fear, like Orwell's, are tempered by his instinct for self-protection; and Winston's bewildered though abject love for his pedantic oppressor is fore-shadowed in the essay:

> The schoolmaster disciplines him either for his own good, or from a love of bullying. Flip and Sambo had chosen to befriend me, and their friend-ship included canings, reproaches, humiliations, which were good for me. . . . Whenever one had the chance to suck up, one did suck up, and at the first smile one's hatred turned into a sort of cringing love.

Finally, Orwell's and Winston's pathetic inability to conform to the inexorable laws is similar in both works. Orwell 'lived among the laws which were absolute, like the law of gravity'; and O'Brien states, 'You are a flaw in the pattern, Winston. You are a stain that must be wiped out.'

Orwell's traumatic experiences at school were extremely influen-tial in determining the events of his later life, and he is undoubtedly thinking of himself when he writes of Kipling, 'Much in his develop-ment is traceable to his having been born in India and having left school early' (II.188).

II

Despite the threats and beatings Orwell won a scholarship to Eton, where he was the contemporary of Connolly, Anthony Powell, Cecil Beaton and Sir Steven Runciman. Aldous Huxley, who taught English and French from 1917 to 1919, was one of Orwell's teachers, and Runciman reports that 'Above all it was Huxley's use of words that entranced us. Eric Blair – the future George Orwell – who was my exact contemporary – would in particular make us note Aldous's phraseology. "That is a word we must remember,"

we used to say to each other.'³⁶ But Huxley's influence was unfortunately limited; and Orwell never studied, learned very little,
got extremely low marks and was 'relatively happy' in a cubicle of
his own:

> For years past I had been resolved – unconsciously at first, but consciously
> later on – that when once my scholarship was won I would 'slack off'
> and cram no longer. This resolve, by the way, was so fully carried out
> that between the ages of thirteen and twenty-two or three I hardly ever
> did a stroke of avoidable work. (IV.363)

There was nothing very unusual about the young Orwell, no
promise of genius, little to suggest that he would become, after
D. H. Lawrence, the most influential writer of the century.

Orwell soon developed a kind of aloofness which left him on good
terms with everyone without being the close friend of any. He was
poor at games, but edited a humorous magazine, *College Days*, and
served in the Officer Training Corps. While he was at Eton, his
father joined the army as a subaltern at the age of sixty, and from
1917 to 1919 took care of mules in an army camp near Marseilles.

Orwell, who had the rare misfortune to be flogged during a
school purge in his final year, when he was eighteen, rejected Eton's
aristocratic values – 'five years in a lukewarm bath of snobbery' –
and did not feel that it was a formative influence in his life. Like
Gordon Comstock, he despised and resented those 'snooty, refined
books on safe painters and safe poets by those moneyed young
beasts who glide so gracefully from Eton to Cambridge and from
Cambridge to the literary reviews'.³⁷ Orwell eventually wrote for
these reviews, but he arrived there by way of Burma and the slums
of Paris and London.

His revulsion from study at Eton determined Orwell's strange
choice of the Burmese Police instead of Cambridge or at least the
political section of the Indian or West African Civil Service. For
Mr A. S. F. Gow, Orwell's classical tutor at Eton, whom Orwell
visited after Burma in 1927 and later corresponded with, has written
to me, in a letter of 1 January 1969, that Orwell's father (an 'elderly

gentleman forever saying "Don't" ') said he 'could not go to a University unless he got a scholarship and . . . there was not the faintest hope of his getting one. . . . He had shown so little taste or aptitude for academic subjects that I doubted whether in any case a University would be worth while for him.' It is not difficult to see why Orwell rejected the recurrence of his schoolboy situation, for at St Cyprian's, 'Either I won my scholarship, or I must leave school at fourteen and . . . [suffer] a kind of ruin I did not know: perhaps the colonies or an office stool.' And even after he won his scholarship he was still considered a failure 'because success was measured not by what you did but by what you *were*'. Orwell states, 'The conviction that it was *not possible* for me to be a success was deep enough to influence my actions till far into adult life. Until I was about thirty [when he published his first book] I always planned my life on the assumption . . . that any major undertaking was bound to fail.'

Orwell's Anglo-Indian background asserted itself when he failed to win a university scholarship, for his father suggested the Burmese Police because of the personal connections the family had 'with the country over three generations. My grandmother lived forty years in Burma' (iv.114). As Ray says of Thackeray, 'The indirect effect of Thackeray's Indian heritage and experience was immense. . . . He grew up in the compact world that Anglo-Indians made for themselves at home, a world ['like a kind of cyst'] in which the Indian service was regarded as a "sacred college of sons and nephews" and there existed "small sympathy for talent without relations".'[38] Weary of the tedious restrictions of school, but influenced by its imperialistic ethos, the youthful Orwell must have been lured by the Kiplingesque exoticism, adventure and freedom of his eastern birthplace:

> For the wind is in the palm-trees, and the temple bells they say:
> Come you back, you British soldier, come you back to Mandalay!

Though none of Orwell's letters from Burma have been published, few of the Burmese files survived the tropical climate and the

Japanese occupation of the country, and it is improbable that any information about Orwell still exists in Burma, the India Office Library in London (Judicial and Procedure file 6079 for the year 1922) provides some factual information about his application and examinations for a position in the Burmese Police.

Orwell left Eton in December 1921 and in January 1922, giving his home address as 20 South Green, Southwold, Suffolk, entered Mr Hope's tutorial establishment to prepare for his competitive examinations. Hope and John Crace, Orwell's master at Eton, supplied the testimonials of good character that Orwell sent in with his application along with the agreement of his father to provide his uniforms. In the summer of 1922 Orwell was examined in English, English History, History and Geography, Mathematics, French, Latin, Greek and Drawing, and earned his highest marks in Latin and his lowest in History and Geography. The old Etonian finished an unimpressive seventh in a class of twenty-nine, but was the best of the three men sent to Burma. On 1 September he was certified as physically fit, and three weeks later barely passed his riding test with 104 points out of a possible 200. Like most of the candidates, Orwell selected Burma as his first choice (the other favourite was the Punjab) and gave as the reason for his preference, 'Have had relations there.' The United Provinces, whose capital was Lucknow, in northern India, was the second choice – 'My father was there for some years' – and his birthplace, Bengal, with its capital, Calcutta, the seat of Indian nationalism, his last option. In October 1922 Orwell was appointed as Probationer in the Burmese Police and was advanced £30, and on the 27th of the month he travelled from Birkenhead to Colombo and Rangoon on the S.S. *Herefordshire*.

In Rangoon Orwell took courses in Burmese, Hindustani, Law and Police Procedure. As a minor official, he served successively in Myaungmya, Twante, Syriam, where he was responsible for the security of an oil refinery, Insein, Katha and Moulmein, where he shot the elephant. Like the young Joyce Cary in Northern Nigeria, Orwell, as Assistant to the District Superintendent in Myaungmya, the capital of Upper Burma, 'was expected to run the office;

supervise the stores of clothing, equipment and ammunition; take charge of the training school for locally recruited constables, as well as the headquarters police station with its strength of thirty to fifty men on active patrol duty and a contingent of escorts for hearings and trials in court. He would also check the night patrols in Myaung-mya, and when his Superintendent was away, touring the sub-divisional headquarters within the District, he would assume general charge.'[39] At Insein, about thirty miles from Rangoon, a colleague was 'rather shattered' to find Orwell's house a kind of chaotic animal farm, with 'goats, geese, ducks and all sorts of things floating about down stairs'.[40] Orwell allowed himself to be undressed by his Burmese servants, whom he sometimes kicked and beat.

After five years of service, Orwell went on home leave from August 1927 until March 1928. Despite the strong tradition of imperialist sentiment in his family and school, he disliked the job of administering the Empire and, as he explains in *The Road to Wigan Pier*, he decided to resign from the Police because of his bitter hatred of imperialism. But his colleague, Roger Beadon, believes there was a personal as well as an ideological reason and that Orwell had to serve 'under a certain District Superintendent of Police who treated him very badly. . . . That was, I think, the main reason why he chucked it and left the Police in 1927.'[41] Orwell may also have suffered under conditions that Conrad describes in 'Outpost of Progress', for contact

> with primitive nature and primitive man, brings sudden and profound trouble into the heart. To the sentiment of being alone of one's kind, to the clear perception of the loneliness of one's thoughts, of one's sensations – to the negation of the habitual, which is safe, there is added the affirmation of the unusual, which is dangerous; a suggestion of things vague, uncontrollable, and repulsive, whose discomposing intrusion excites the imagination and tries the civilised nerves of the foolish and the wise alike.[42]

Orwell asked for permission to resign as Assistant Superintendent of Police as of 1 January 1928. Though his superiors were annoyed because he gave no reason for leaving, they approved his request, which terminated the unhappy career that he recorded in 'A Hanging', 'Shooting an Elephant' and *Burmese Days*.

Orwell returned from the East as a rather frayed sahib, and his sister reports, 'I suppose being used to a lot of servants in India [i.e. Burma] he'd become terribly – to our minds – untidy. Whenever he smoked a cigarette he threw the end down on the floor – and the match – and expected other people to sweep them up.'[43] Orwell soon went native in England just as he had done in Burma. In the autumn of 1927 he bought tramps' clothing in a pawnshop and made the first of his many expeditions, during the next five years, among the poor and outcast of London.

In the spring of 1928 he rented a shabby room in a working-class quarter of Paris, and published his first article, on censorship in England, in Henri Barbusse's weekly newspaper, *Monde*. In February 1929 Orwell fell ill with pneumonia and spent several weeks in the Hôpital Cochin in Paris as a charity patient and mute specimen for medical students. He writes in 'How the Poor Die' (1946) that 'when I entered the ward at the Hôpital X, I was conscious of a strange feeling of familiarity. What the scene reminded me of, of course, was the reeking, pain-filled hospitals of the nineteenth century' – just as St Cyprian's had reminded him of the squalid Victorian schools in Dickens.

As a non-paying inmate, Orwell endured the barbaric conditions and grim treatment that foreshadow the wartime hospitals of Spain and the torture chamber of *1984*. After a crude and ineffectual cupping (the hot glass was popped on the chest causing a huge yellow blister and 'drew out about a dessert-spoonful of dark-coloured blood'), 'I lay down again, humiliated, disgusted and frightened by the thing that had been done to me. . . . One wants to live, of course, indeed one only stays alive by virtue of the fear of death' (v.225,228). Like Winston Smith, Orwell remained alive in Paris for only negative reasons.

In the summer of 1929 Orwell wrote several short stories and two apprentice novels, which he could not publish. When the last of his money was stolen, he did not call upon his favourite aunt, who was living in Paris at that time, but pawned all his clothes and worked for ten weeks as a dishwasher in a luxurious but filthy hotel. His experiences among the poor of the two capitals were the subject of his first book, *Down and Out in Paris and London*, which was rejected by Cape and Faber, and published by Gollancz in 1933 under the pseudonym of George Orwell. This name was selected from a list that included P. S. Burton (the name he used while tramping), Kenneth Miles and H. Lewis Allways.

Orwell left Paris at the end of 1929, and before his book was published he tutored a retarded boy near his parents' home in Southwold, a resort on the Suffolk coast, picked hops in Kent and taught in two small private schools at Hayes and Uxbridge. In the first school he thrashed a boy who was blowing up a frog with a bicycle pump. The backward boy may have been the subject of his lost short story, 'An Idiot', and the last two experiences were incorporated into *A Clergyman's Daughter*, which begins in a Suffolk vicarage.

From 1930 to 1935 Orwell contributed to the *Adelphi*, a magazine which had been founded by Middleton Murry in 1923 and was now edited by Orwell's close friend, Sir Richard Rees. Orwell began the prolonged, indiscriminate reviewing of books which brought in three or four pounds a week and which he described in 'Confessions of a Book Reviewer' (1946) as 'a quite exceptionally thankless, irritating and exhausting job' (IV.183). Orwell's journalistic output was enormous, and in less than twenty years he produced more than seven hundred articles in addition to his books.

In October 1934 Orwell took a part-time job in a Hampstead bookshop (his presence there is now commemorated by a plaque), worked there for a year and a half, and wrote about this experience in 'Bookshop Memories' and *Keep the Aspidistra Flying*. In January 1936 he was commissioned by the Left Book Club to write about economic and social conditions in the depressed industrial regions of northern England, gave up his job in the bookshop and spent the next three months gathering material for *The Road to Wigan Pier*. In the spring he moved to the village of Wallington, near Baldock in Hertfordshire, where he finished the book, did some vegetable farming and kept some barnyard animals which he later portrayed in *Animal Farm*.

In June 1936 Orwell married Eileen O'Shaughnessy, a rather frail but attractive graduate student in psychology at the University of London who was three years younger than he was. Elisaveta Fen describes her as 'sophisticated, fastidious, highly intelligent and intellectual. . . . She was tall and slender . . . with blue eyes and dark brown, naturally wavy hair.'[44]

Orwell went to Spain in December, five months after the outbreak of the Civil War that began, like the October Revolution, with cinemas open and visitors strolling in the streets. He did not attend literary congresses; did not meet other writers like Hemingway and Dos Passos, Pablo Neruda and Rafael Alberti, who often gathered at the Hotel Florida on the Gran Via in Madrid; and did not join the more famous organizations, like Malraux's Escadre España and the International Brigade, which attracted most foreign fighters. Instead, Orwell enlisted in the rather obscure and ill-equipped Trotskyist POUM militia at the Lenin barracks in Barcelona, where 'the shabby clothes and the gay-coloured revolutionary posters, the universal use of the word "comrade", and the anti-Fascist ballads printed on flimsy paper and sold for a penny' created a special atmosphere of international solidarity (II.256). Eileen arrived in Spain in February 1937, visited the front for a few days and then worked at the Independent Labour Party office in Barcelona.

After a week of so-called training, Orwell became an ordinary soldier in the revolutionary army and fought with the ILP contingent on the Aragon front in north-east Spain. He endured the boredom and hunger of static trench warfare in a freezing climate until he was shot through the throat by a Fascist sniper on 10 May. When he began to recover from his wound the following month, he volunteered to return to battle. But POUM was suddenly declared illegal in mid-June and the Orwells, investigated and hunted by the Communist police, barely managed to cross the French frontier into safety. These events were the subject of what is perhaps his greatest book, *Homage to Catalonia*, which Gollancz refused to publish before a word was written because of Orwell's attack on Stalin's Communists, just as Kingsley Martin, the editor of the *New Statesman*, refused to publish Orwell's reviews of books about the Civil War.

In March 1938 Orwell became ill with tuberculosis, a recurrence of his childhood disease, and was unable to travel to India to write for the Lucknow *Pioneer* and do research for a book on the subcontinent. Thanks to an anonymous gift of £300 from the novelist L. H. Myers, Orwell and his wife were able to spend the winter in Marrakech, Morocco, where he wrote *Coming Up For Air*. His years in Henley-on-Thames, the site of the famous regatta, provided the background for the nostalgic childhood scenes in that novel. In his essay 'Marrakech', Orwell concentrated more on colonial exploitation than on the exotic atmosphere, and wrote that 'For nine-tenths of the people the reality of life is an endless, back-breaking struggle to wring a little food out of an eroded soil' (1.390). Unfortunately, Marrakech did not improve the Orwells' health and they were not much stronger when they returned to England in the spring of 1939. In June Orwell's father died of cancer at the age of 82.

When the war that Orwell had anticipated for so long finally broke out in September, he tried to enlist in the army just as his elderly father had done in the previous war, but was rejected as medically unfit. In his excellent essay on Orwell, his Tory friend Anthony Powell writes: 'The bad health that prevented him from taking an active part in the war was a terrible blow to Orwell. He saw himself as a man of action and felt passionately about the things for which the country was fighting. When he heard Evelyn Waugh was serving with a Commando Unit, he said: "Why can't someone on the Left ever do something like that?" '[45] Orwell eventually utilized his military experience in Spain by becoming a rather ineffectual sergeant in the St John's Wood Home Guard battalion in May 1940 and, with his publisher Fredric Warburg, marched to imaginary battle under the Old School Tie. Warburg reports that, while commanding a mortar drill, 'Orwell had not seen that it was the practice, not the drill bomb that had been loaded. . . . The mortar, not being dug in, recoiled. Private Smith lost virtually all his front teeth, top and bottom, while Private Jones was unconscious for at least 24 hours.'[46]

George Woodcock, who met Orwell early in the War, describes him as 'a tall, thin, angular man with worn Gothic features accentuated by the deep vertical furrows that ran down the cheeks and across the corners of the mouth. The thinness of his lips was emphasized by a very narrow line of dark moustache. . . . The general gauntness of his looks was accentuated by the deep sockets from which his eyes looked out, always rather sadly.'[47] And John Morris adds that 'his most striking features were his luxuriant and unruly hair and the strange expression in his eyes, a combination of benevolence and fanaticism'.[48] Orwell always wore the same clothes: an old tweed sports jacket with leather patches at the elbows, baggy corduroy trousers, dark shirt with shaggy wool tie, rough unpolished shoes and a grimy trenchcoat. He took a childish pleasure in adopting working-class habits like (rather inexpertly) rolling his own slack but strong cigarettes and drinking tea from his saucer.

In January 1941 Orwell wrote the first of his fifteen wartime 'London Letters' for the *Partisan Review*. Beginning in August, he spent more than two years as Talks Producer for the Indian Section of the BBC, and in his flat, monotonous voice, which had been affected by his Spanish bullet wound, Orwell broadcast propaganda to Anglophile Asians. Orwell's distinguished contributors included E. M. Forster, T. S. Eliot and Herbert Read, and two of his programmes were published in *Talking to India* (1943). He used his BBC experiences as the basis for the bureaucratic Ministry of Truth in *1984*.

In November 1943 Orwell left the BBC and became literary editor of the *Tribune*, which was edited by the Labour MP Aneurin Bevan. On that newspaper Orwell began his amusing and idiosyncratic 'As I Please' column, which he continued for the next four years, his subjects ranging from the New Year's Honours List to the ugliest building in the world. 'The *Tribune* is not perfect,' Orwell later wrote, but it seemed to represent his values and beliefs. 'I do think it is the only existing weekly paper that makes a genuine effort to be both progressive and humane – that is, to combine a radical Socialist policy with a respect for freedom of speech and a civilised attitude towards literature and the arts' (III.409). Though Orwell was a superb columnist, he was less successful as an editor. Woodcock sternly reports that Orwell 'found it extremely difficult to return an article with a coldly-worded rejection slip . . . and published a great deal of shoddy trash by young writers who had no promise to fulfil'.[49]

Orwell completed *Animal Farm* in February 1944 and was shocked to have it rejected for political reasons by Gollancz (who had refused to publish *Homage to Catalonia*), Cape and Faber (who had also rejected his first book). T. S. Eliot, a director of Faber, softened the blow by praising the literary merits of the satire against the Russian ally: 'We agree that it is a distinguished piece of writing, that the fable is very skilfully handled, and that the narrative keeps one's interest on its own plane – and that is something very few authors have achieved since *Gulliver*. . . . But we have no conviction . . . that this is the right point of view from which to criticise the political situation at the present time.'[50]

Orwell was quite naturally frustrated and angry, and in July wrote to his agent, Leonard Moore, that if Warburg did not publish it, 'I am not going to tout it round further publishers, which wastes time & may lead to nothing, but shall publish it myself. . . . I have already half-arranged to do so & have got the necessary financial backing' (III.187). Though Orwell made arrangements with his friend Paul Potts at the Whitman Press, who had the necessary paper despite the wartime shortages, *Animal Farm* was in fact published by Warburg in August 1945, at a crucial moment in world history. In the previous four months, Roosevelt, Mussolini and Hitler had died, Churchill had been voted out of office, Germany had surrendered and, on 6 August, the atomic bomb had exploded over Hiroshima. Of the Big Three, only Stalin still survived.

That month was also a turning point in Orwell's history, for half a million copies of *Animal Farm* were sold through the American

Book-of-the-Month Club and he became financially successful for the first time in his life. After his death the book was made into an extremely effective animated cartoon in 1954, and by 1972 sales in hardcover and paperback editions had reached eleven million.

But Orwell's literary success was marred by a personal tragedy. He and his wife, who were unable to have children of their own, had adopted a one-month-old baby in June 1944 and named him Richard Horatio Blair. (He is now a farmer in England.) In February 1945 Orwell went to France and then to Germany as a war correspondent for the *Observer*. While he was abroad, Eileen, who had been in poor health throughout the War (the Orwells had given up part of their scanty rations so that 'other people' could have more), underwent an operation to arrest the fall of red corpuscles in her blood. As the anaesthetic was being administered, she suddenly died.

The adoption of Richard, the unexpected death of Eileen, the tremendous success of *Animal Farm* and a serious deterioration in his own health completely transformed Orwell's life within a few months. Despite, or perhaps because of, the death of his wife, Orwell refused to give up his adopted son. He kept a goat in his backyard in 1945 to provide milk for Richard, who was cared for by several housekeepers until Orwell's younger sister, Avril, came to live with him in 1946.

Orwell first visited the island of Jura in the Hebrides in September 1945 and returned to live there in the winter of 1946. There was no telephone or electricity in his house on the far end of the island at Barnhill, which required strenuous maintenance and could be reached only by a rough cart-track eight miles long. Life on Jura was almost like camping out. His wife's death, and his own stern asceticism and distaste for social life, created in him a perverse compulsion to live the arduous and exhausting existence on the rainy island, far from medical assistance and in a country that he, like Samuel Johnson, professed to dislike. The suicidal decision to live on Jura, where he wrote *1984*, hastened the terminal phase of his grave illness (he could speak, like Pope, of 'this long disease, my Life') and brought him to an early death at 46.

III

When the fatalistic Orwell anticipates *1984* and asks, 'Is it perhaps childish or morbid to terrify oneself with visions of a totalitarian future?' (II.259), his adjectival alternatives suggest the connection between the two autobiographical strains of his ultimate totalitarian vision: his experiences at school and the terrifying disease of his last years.

Like Lawrence, Orwell seems to have had defective lungs since boyhood, for in 'Such, Such Were the Joys', he writes, 'After the age of ten, I was seldom in good health. . . . I had defective bronchial tubes and a lesion in one lung which was not discovered till many years later.' Though Orwell writes, 'I do not think I can be imagining the fact that we were underfed, when I remember the lengths we would go in order to steal food,' the school authorities felt his chronic cough was caused by 'overeating', and their failure to give him medical treatment intensified the disease that tormented him for the rest of his life and eventually caused his death. The hot and humid Burmese climate ruined his health; he was hospitalized for pneumonia in February 1929 and again in December 1933; was shot through the throat in May 1937; had tuberculosis in March 1938; and was rejected as unfit for military service in 1939 because of bronchiectasis.

Orwell believed, like Keats, that 'Until we are sick, we understand not.' The relation between Orwell's disease and his art was very close, and he states that 'writing a book is a horrible, exhausting struggle, like a long bout of some painful illness' (I.7). This is particularly true of *1984*, whose central metaphor is disease and whose main character undergoes an operation, a kind of electric lobotomy, and is 'cured'. There is a strong sense of impending death throughout the novel – 'from the moment of declaring war on the Party it was better to think of yourself as a corpse' – as well as a powerful death-wish, for the novel ends as Winston imagines 'the long-hoped-for bullet was entering his brain'. As Orwell writes of *1984* in October 1948, 'I think it is a good idea but the execution

would have been better if I had not written it under the influence of
TB' (IV.448).

1984 was begun in August 1946 and finished 27 months later
in November 1948, and Orwell was seriously ill for much of that
time. He was sick in bed in April 1947, ill in May and September,
and forced into bed again in October. In the summer he and
Richard were shipwrecked in a dangerous whirlpool off Jura and
were lucky to be rescued by a passing fisherman. He entered a
tuberculosis sanatorium near Glasgow in December 1947 and
remained there until June 1948; suffered a relapse in September and
October, and was seriously ill in November and December 1948.
He entered another sanatorium in the Cotswolds in January 1949,
corrected the proofs there, and was in hospital in Gloucestershire
and London for the last year of his life. His letters during this period
reflect the gravity of his disease, which plays such an important part
in the novel:

> May 1947: I have really been in most wretched health this year ever
> since about January (my chest as usual) and can't quite shake it off.
> (IV.329)

> January 1948: I am still really very ill & weak, & on getting here I found
> I had lost 1½ stone. . . . I was glad to get away before Xmas so as not to
> be a death's head. (IV.391-2)

Most of Orwell's letters are strangely impersonal, but they become
extraordinarily moving during the last months of his life when he
faces the gravity of his disease with a fine courage. He was devoted
to his adopted son, Richard, and poignantly writes:

> I am so afraid of his growing away from me, or getting to think of me
> as just a person who is always lying down & can't play. Of course
> children can't understand illness. He used to come to me & say 'Where
> have you hurt yourself?' (IV.479)

In May 1949 he admits:

> I am in most ghastly health. . . . When the picture is taken I am afraid
> there is not much doubt it will show that both lungs have deteriorated

badly. I asked the doctor recently whether she thought I would survive, & she wouldn't go further than saying she didn't know. . . . But I want to get a clear idea of *how long* I am likely to last, & not just be jollied along the way doctors usually do. (IV.500)

In August he announces, rather surprisingly:

I intend getting married again (to Sonia) when I am once again in the land of the living, if I ever am. I suppose everyone will be horrified. (IV.505–6)

A tuberculosis specialist has noted, 'It is often astonishing to behold the sinking man make plans for the future, engage in new enterprises . . . or, as I have seen, arranging for his marriage a few days before his death.'[51] In September Orwell was transferred to University College Hospital in London; and in October he married Sonia Brownell, who was born in India and was a secretary on Cyril Connolly's magazine, *Horizon*, from 1945 to 1950. Orwell wrote that month, 'I am still very weak & ill, but I think better on the whole. . . . It will probably be a long time before I can get out of bed' (IV.508).

Orwell did not live to enjoy the success of *1984*, which was published in June 1949. It has since sold more than eleven million copies, and in 1956 was made into a film with Edmund O'Brien as Winston Smith. Orwell started an article on Evelyn Waugh (see IV.512–13), and had plans for a long essay on the political novels of Joseph Conrad and for a novel set in 1945. He seemed better in January 1950 and made plans to enter a Swiss sanatorium. But he died of pulmonary tuberculosis on 21 January, and was buried in the churchyard of All Saints in Sutton Courtenay, Berkshire.

The details of physical, especially respiratory, pain are one of the most striking features of *1984* and are clearly based on personal experience. As Winston is startled out of sleep each morning by the piercing voice of the telescreen, he is 'doubled up by a violent coughing fit which . . . emptied his lungs so completely that he could only begin breathing again by lying on his back and taking a series of deep gasps'. When the Thought Police invade the forbidden room and smash Julia in the solar plexus, *Winston* knew 'the terrible, agonizing pain which was there all the while but could not be suffered yet, because before all else it was necessary to be able to breathe'. The tortures in Room 101 – 'you could not feel anything, except pain and the foreknowledge of pain' – where Winston is conveyed by attendants in white coats who drug him with a hypodermic syringe, strap him flat on his back and connect him with wires to a machine, come directly from Orwell's awful years in hospitals,[52] rather than from memories of Sambo's study, as West suggests. When O'Brien turns up the instrument of torture, 'The air tore into his lungs and issued again in deep groans ... [and he had] a vivid mental picture of the vertebrae snapping apart and the spinal fluid dripping out of them.' West writes that Orwell 'seems to relish the murky and the horrible',[53] but it would be truer to say he is unable to escape his own physical deterioration and sense of impending death. Even in *Animal Farm*, weak lungs cause Boxer's collapse, and 'a thin stream of blood trickled out of his mouth'.

After the torture, Winston looks in the mirror and poignantly sees that 'A bowed, grey-colored, skeleton-like thing was coming toward him.... A feeling of pity for his ruined body overcame him ... it was the body of a man of sixty, suffering from some malignant disease,' like the 'death's head' who had lost more than twenty pounds. Just as Winston 'recognizes himself as a dead man' but feels it is 'important to stay alive as long as possible', so Orwell writes in one of his last letters: 'Don't think I am making up my mind to peg out. On the contrary, I have the strongest reasons for wanting to stay alive' (IV.500).

Orwell's disease is also reflected in the novel in two less obvious ways. One of the weaknesses of the book, a fault not common in his earlier novels, is Orwell's description of characters' feelings in terms of crude physiological responses. Most of these physical effects result from pain and fear: noise 'set one's teeth on edge and bristled the hair', Winston's heart turns 'to ice and his bowels to water', his 'teeth chatter and knees knock'. Orwell belabours this technique because of his inevitable preoccupation with his own deteriorating body, reflected in Winston's belief 'that in moments of crisis one is . . . always [fighting] against one's own body'. More significantly, Winston's frightening vision of a sinking ship and drowning people 'coming up for air' becomes the most important *leitmotif* in the novel and symbolizes the terror of helpless humanity. This image is metamorphosed in Winston's mind as he pictures himself at the bottom of the sea and repeatedly imagines first his family and then himself as drowning victims, unable to breathe and dying of suffocation: 'If you have come up from deep water it is not cowardly to fill your lungs with air.' The drowning sensation is directly related not only to the cause of death from tuberculosis, but also to the feeling of a post-operative patient regaining consciousness after anaesthesia. When Winston awakes in Room 101, 'He had the impression of swimming up into this room from some . . . under-water world far beneath it.'

The personal elements in *1984* intensify its considerable power, for Orwell is able to fuse his primitive fears of childhood vulner-ability, expressed in 'Such, Such', with his intuition of extermination camp atrocities, the central trauma of our time. This raw revelation of his illness has, like the last letters of Keats and Lawrence, the impact of a final testament.[54]

The dominant pattern of Orwell's life that emerges from 'Such, Such' is the series of self-induced masochistic impulses for a higher cause that testifies to his compulsive need to expiate his intense childhood guilt by self-punishment: at St Cyprian's; in the Burmese Police; among scullions and beggars; in squalid doss-houses and inside mines; with the ragged, ill-equipped army of the Spanish Republic; in propagandistic drudgery for the wartime BBC (a 'whoreshop and lunatic asylum'); in thankless and exhausting political polemics; and finally in that mad and suicidal sojourn on the bleak and isolated island of Jura. In *Wigan Pier* Orwell states that he was haunted by a sense of political guilt that derived from his years as a colonial oppressor. But it seems that the cause of this guilt, which he could never extinguish, occurred earlier than

Orwell suggests and had its deep roots in his childhood. Though this masochistic strain persisted, Orwell's writing is manifest proof of his ability to transcend this personal guilt by channelling it into effective political thought and action. His own guilt and suffering led to a compassion for the suffering of others, to an ethic of responsibility.

2 The Essays

ORWELL'S ESSAYS form five major groups: autobiographical, literary, political, sociological and cultural. 'Such, Such Were the Joys', 'Shooting an Elephant', 'A Hanging', 'How the Poor Die', 'Bookshop Memories', 'Marrakech', 'Confessions of a Book Reviewer' and 'Why I Write' comprise the cluster of autobiographical essays. There are the literary essays on novelists who influenced him: Dickens, Gissing and Koestler; and on those whom he admired but criticized for their reactionary political views, for Orwell believed that 'enjoyment can overwhelm disapproval, even though one clearly recognizes that one is enjoying something inimical' (IV.221). These essays are on Swift, Tolstoy, Kipling, Yeats, Wells, Wodehouse and Henry Miller. The political essays concern literature and totalitarianism and are closely connected to *1984*: 'The Prevention of Literature', 'Writers and Leviathan', 'Politics and the English Language', 'James Burnham and the Managerial Revolution' and 'Looking Back on the Spanish War'. Orwell's essays on the sociology of England are 'England Your England', 'The English People', 'Poetry and the Microphone', 'Notes on Nationalism' and 'Anti-Semitism in Britain'. His criticism of popular culture is closely related to *Coming Up For Air* and includes 'Raffles and Miss Blandish', 'Decline of the English Murder', 'Boys' Weeklies', 'The Art of Donald McGill', 'Riding Down From Bangor' and 'Good Bad Books'. A discussion of some representative essays – in which Orwell writes about himself as well as his subject, expresses his characteristic ideas, and reveals his values and beliefs more directly than in his novels – provides a framework for the analysis of his major works.

I Charles Dickens (1939)

'Charles Dickens', the longest of Orwell's essays, was one of the earliest critical studies of the novelist and is still valuable for its freshness, vigour and suggestiveness. The essay considers many of the approaches to Dickens that were later explored by critics in full-length books: Dickens's attitudes to society, class, money, sex and politics; his literary techniques, comedy, imagery, use of detail and creation of character through caricature. But the essay is also important for what it tells us about Orwell, for he says as much about what he is trying to do in his own work as about Dickens.

Orwell begins with a negative definition of Dickens, who was neither a 'proletarian' nor a 'revolutionary' writer. Though bourgeois, he was 'a subversive writer, a radical, one might truthfully say a rebel'. Though Dickens was not revolutionary *'in the accepted sense'*, Orwell feels that, like Blake, he understood what living in a capitalist society means. Orwell explores the paradoxical fact that the major, radical theme of Dickens's novels ('the central problem – how to prevent power from being abused') is at variance with Dickens's bourgeois solutions. One force behind Orwell's analysis is the need to reconcile his sense of Dickens's greatness as a novelist with his feeble political thought. One of his purposes in writing the essay is to use his study of Dickens to establish his opposition to propagandistic literature. Throughout the essay Orwell implicitly measures his own talents as a writer against the genius and achievement of Dickens. The essay demonstrates how completely Orwell integrated his imaginative with his practical and political life, for he wrote his most successful novels when he discovered a medium that used literary art to convey political ideas.

Orwell's characterization of Dickens as a writer who combines a radical criticism of society with a persistent longing for a traditional way of life is very close to his own nostalgic feelings in *Coming Up For Air*. Orwell's observation that 'the very people he attacked have swallowed him so completely that he has become a national institution himself', reminds us that the same is now true of Orwell. His remark that 'Before I was ten years old I was having Dickens ladled down my throat by schoolmasters in whom even at that age I could see a strong resemblance to Mr Creakle' is ironic in several senses. For *Animal Farm* is also taught in schools today, and not always in the spirit that Orwell intended. It is in the nature of English culture, Orwell suggests, to absorb and domesticate radical literature.

Orwell is attracted to Dickens because the novelist tried to understand how human suffering comes about and how it can be overcome. This central problem of the abuse of power became the theme of *Animal Farm*. It is obvious to Orwell that people are oppressed by leaders and by institutions. The crux is what the solution to this problem should be: 'There is always a new tyrant waiting to take over from the old – generally not quite so bad, but still a tyrant.' Orwell thinks that two positions are tenable: the moralistic and the revolutionary. The revolutionary supposes that you can improve human nature by changing the system, while Dickens, the moralist, believes that the world will change only when men have a change of heart. Orwell's technique is to demonstrate fully the weakness of Dickens's moralistic attitude so that, paradoxically, he can emphasize the value of Dickens's idea of decency, a moral concept that Orwell adopted in his own work.

Orwell's discussion of the novels themselves, therefore, combines an exercise in debunking and a warm appreciation of the enjoyment to be gained from Dickens. Orwell balances and opposes Dickens's strengths and weaknesses. He is intellectually shallow but emotionally profound; he savagely attacks social evils, but accepts the social inequalities of his age and makes no constructive criticism of Victorian society – an accusation that was later made against Orwell. Dickens did not really know the working class, and portrayed them either as the rough and alien boys of his time in the blacking factory, or as feudal servants. Orwell contrasts the loving personable servants in Dickens's novels with the reality of the 'slavey drudging fourteen hours a day in the basement kitchen'. Orwell shows that though his invention is brilliant and his characters memorable, Dickens is ignorant of all social classes but his own – 'the London commercial bourgeoisie and their hangers-on' – and that he lacks detailed knowledge of the major occupations and institutions of his day.

Dickens's novels raise all kinds of questions about education, industrial exploitation and the legal system, and yet his answers seem to reveal 'an enormous deficiency': the lack of intellectual curiosity and the absence of an ideal of work. In fact, Dickens does not write at all about work, and though his novels show men and women struggling toward self-knowledge and the fulfilment of ambition, the goal to which they aspire is a kind of cosy and blissful family life. Orwell devotes several pages to demonstrating the feebleness of Dickens's 'featherbed respectability' and concludes that these intellectually unacceptable solutions to social injustices and human cruelty are the substance of Dickens's 'message'. It is interesting to note that Orwell illustrates this aspect of Dickens so fully, for the idea of the secure, old-fashioned family also occurs in his own work, not as a solution to injustice and cruelty, but as an idealized alternative in an earlier and happier age.

After dealing with the negative side of Dickens, Orwell briefly but accurately defines the genius of the novelist, and reverses the traditional positions of moralist and revolutionary. Dickens's 'fertility of invention', his use of details to create characters of monstrous proportions, the play of his imagination, unregulated by any intellectual framework or higher creative purpose, are qualities that make his creations endure: 'They are monsters, but they exist. . . . Dickens is obviously a writer whose parts are greater than his wholes. He is all fragments, all details – rotten architecture, but wonderful gargoyles.'

Orwell believes that the driving force behind the comedy is 'the consciousness of "having something to say". He is always preaching a sermon, and that is the final secret of his inventiveness. For you can only create if you can *care*. . . . A joke worth laughing at always has an idea behind it, and usually a subversive idea.' The moralist turns out to be the true radical, and 'most revolutionaries are potential Tories, because they imagine that everything can be put right by altering the *shape* of society'. Dickens has 'not even a clear grasp of the nature of the society he is attacking, only an emotional perception that something is wrong'. But Orwell feels that emotional responses to evil are more trustworthy than revolutionary programmes, for it is an illusion to think that society can be perfected by changing its form: there are some kinds of evil that will never disappear. Orwell's observation that 'The vagueness of Dickens's discontent is the mark of its permanence' applies equally to *Animal Farm* and *1984*. In Dickens, however, there is a force that mitigates this pessimistic vision: his 'native generosity of mind . . . [which] is probably the central secret of his popularity' and which enables him to 'express in a comic, simplified and therefore memorable form the native decency of the common man'.

Orwell, who inherited Dickens's belief in decency, was particularly impressed by *Hard Times* (1854). Stephen Blackpool was probably Orwell's first introduction to the industrial working class; and the utilitarians, Bounderby and Gradgrind, are the precursors of the totalitarian inquisitors in *1984*. In this novel Orwell employs Dickens's technique of using a working-class character to represent the spirit of ordinary humanity, for just as Mr Sleary maintains that 'people must be amuthed', so Winston Smith is revived when he hears the singing of the red-armed prole washerwoman.

A consideration of how far a good novel should be committed to conveying a political idea is at the root of Orwell's discussion of Dickens. Orwell begins his essay with a question that leads to the choice between moralist and revolutionary: to whom does Dickens belong, to the bourgeois conservative or to the Marxist? Orwell resolves this question by asserting that Dickens's genius endures precisely because it is based not on ideology, but on a belief in the fundamental decency and the brotherhood of man. But the conclusion of the essay is rather weak. The violence of Orwell's opposition to the 'smelly little orthodoxies' of political writers suggests that he is aware that the humanist position is weak. Though his affinity with Dickens is considerable, his analysis reveals the wide divergence of their ideas. Modern political events weakened Orwell's belief in man until, in his later works, decency and goodness become the attributes not of heroes, but of victims.

II INSIDE THE WHALE (1940)

In 'Inside the Whale', the title-essay of his first volume of essays, which was published soon after the Second World War broke out, Orwell defines his own place in contemporary literature by means of a sympathetic contrast to Henry Miller, and to the main literary traditions of the twenties and thirties. Though Miller's *Tropic of Cancer* (1931) seems to be the very antithesis of Orwell's work, it is set in the proletarian Paris of the 1920s and describes 'bug-ridden rooms in working men's hotels, fights, drinking bouts, cheap brothels, Russian refugees, cadging, swindling and temporary jobs, the whole atmosphere of the poor quarters in Paris as a foreigner sees them' – and as Orwell saw them in 1928–29 and wrote about them in *Down and Out in Paris and London*. Like Miller, Orwell had no connection with the brilliant literary and artistic world of Paris before the crash, the world of Joyce, Hemingway, Fitzgerald, Picasso, Braque and Miró; and *Tropic of Cancer*, for all its obscenity and amorality, represents the *kind* of novel Orwell might have written about the inane, squalid facts of everyday life in Paris. For Miller's whole atmosphere was deeply familiar to Orwell: 'You have all the while the feeling that these things are happening to *you*.'

What distinguishes Miller from Orwell and from most of the writers of the thirties is his passive, non-political attitude, his rather indifferent though realistic acceptance of the world as it is. In the second part of the essay Orwell explains Miller's escape from the current literary fashion by discussing the 'message' of the major

English writers since the Great War. Housman's cynical strain and bitter defiant paganism, his implied sexual revolt and his personal grievance against God, made him the most influential poet just after the war. But Housman was soon eclipsed by the more experimental writers of the 1920s – Joyce, Eliot, Pound, Lawrence – who replaced the Georgian poets' 'beauty of Nature' with a 'tragic sense of life'. Both schools were escapist, though in different ways. Housman and the Georgians evoked the thatched roofs and muscular smiths in the buried villages of pre-industrial England; while the more *avant-garde* writers looked 'to Rome, to Byzantium, to Montparnasse, to Mexico, to the Etruscans, to the subconscious, to the solar plexus – to anywhere except the place where things were actually happening'.

The Auden–Spender school of the thirties revolted against the pessimistic and reactionary outlook of their predecessors[1] and introduced a 'serious purpose' into literature. By 1930 traditional values like religion, the family, patriotism and the Empire had lost their significance; and during the struggle against Fascism, English intellectuals turned toward the patriotism of the deracinated and came under the influence of Communist ideology. But they did not realize, as Orwell did in Spain when he saw the bodies of murdered men, that 'the Communist movement in western Europe, [which] began as a movement for the violent overthrow of capitalism, degenerated within a few years into an instrument for Russian foreign policy'.

These English writers, who grew up in the land of liberalism and habeas corpus, were able to accept and even condone 'the purge-and-Ogpu [secret police] side of the Russian regime and the horrors of the First Five Year Plan' in which many thousands of people were killed, because they were incapable of understanding it. The phrase 'necessary murder' from Auden's poem 'Spain' 'could only be written by a person to whom murder is at most a *word*'. Thus, Left-wing literature, though it deliberately concerned itself with the politics of the contemporary world, was also, in a fundamental sense, escapist and could not recognize the Russian horrors.

In the final section, Orwell returns to Henry Miller, who shares his own sense of the impending ruin of modern civilization, 'only he does not feel called upon to do anything about it'. Orwell agrees with Miller that remaining metaphorically inside the whale and unaffected by the tyranny and fear in the modern world is an attractive, comfortable declaration of irresponsibility; and he even tolerates this attitude because it expresses the feelings of most people. But Orwell is unable to take this position himself because 'we are moving into an age of totalitarian dictatorships – an age in which freedom of thought will be at first a deadly sin and later on a meaningless abstraction. The autonomous individual is going to be stamped out of existence.'

By foreshadowing the frightening theme of *1984*, Orwell places himself in opposition to the three groups of writers he has discussed. He shares the Georgians' love of the English countryside at the turn of the century, the experimentalists' pessimism and desire to escape to an earlier and happier world, the Leftists' serious purpose and hatred of Fascism – and Miller's sense of the approaching cataclysm. But because the individual, like Winston Smith, is doomed to destruction, Orwell feels compelled to continue the fight and to warn the world – even if his warning does no good. Orwell was never part of a movement and never founded a school. He remained a solitary and individualistic writer whose reputation and stature are based on his personal example as well as on his literary legacy.

III ENGLAND YOUR ENGLAND (1941)

'England Your England' is the opening section of the somewhat propagandistic *The Lion and the Unicorn: Socialism and the English Genius*, the first in a series of Searchlight booklets which offered socialistic solutions to wartime problems. It was later reprinted separately and stands as an independent work. The title, which is not used ironically as it is by Lawrence in his story, 'England, My England', comes from W. E. Henley's patriotic poem, 'For England's Sake' (1892):

> What have I done for you,
>   England, my England?
> What is there I would not do,
>   England, my own?

Orwell analyses the distinctive cultural characteristics and class structure of England, and contrasts the English belief in justice and objective truth to the power-worship and terrorism of the Fascist enemies. As in 'Inside the Whale', he implicitly suggests his own character and ideals through his definition of the positive and negative qualities of English life.

Orwell begins with a concrete description of the sounds, the smells and the surfaces of things one feels when returning to England from abroad: 'The beer is bitterer, the coins are heavier, the grass is greener, the advertisements are more blatant. The crowds in the big towns, with their mild knobby faces, their bad teeth and gentle manners, are different from a European crowd.' He then expresses these differences through some generalizations about the English. They are not gifted in music or the visual arts; dislike abstract thought; are snobbish, xenophobic and hypocritical (particularly in the Empire, which often brings out the worst aspects of the English); value privacy and individual liberty; and, though their religious belief is weak, have a deep respect for morality and legality. Their gentleness is manifested in a hatred of war and militarism, and a tendency to support the weaker side. Their defeats are more familiar than their victories, and 'the most stirring battle-poem in English [Tennyson's 'Charge of the Light Brigade'] is about a brigade of cavalry which charged in the wrong direction' and was massacred. Just as artistic insensibility is balanced by a great literature and a lack of intellectuality by a gift for instinctive action, so gentleness is compounded with barbarities like flogging and hanging, and individual liberty with rigid class distinctions and a gross inequality of wealth and privilege.

The tone of the essay always balances Orwell's two ostensibly opposite purposes: to encourage his compatriots in wartime by celebrating their distinctness and their merits as a nation; and at the same time to attack the political system from a Socialist point of view. Orwell skilfully uses commonly accepted generalizations to produce convincing conclusions and is deliberately provocative, for he sceptically calls British democracy 'less of a fraud than it sometimes appears'.

Orwell suggests that England is currently engaged in a war not because of historical inevitability or the aggressive policies of the European dictators, but because of the decay of ability in the English ruling class and the disastrous foreign policy of the thirties, which Auden called 'a low, dishonest decade'. Just as the English writers of the thirties refused to see the Russian reality and supported Communism because it opposed Fascism, so the English statesmen of that time refused to notice the changes that were occurring all around them and accepted Fascism because it was hostile to Communism. England (and France) remained strictly neutral during the Spanish Civil War and allowed Germany and Italy to fight in Spain and win Franco's war against the Left-wing Republicans; and they never realized that this victory would have a disastrous effect on their own policies and interests. Though the ruling class were morally sound, they were 'tossed to and fro between their incomes and their principles' (any rich man has less to fear from Fascism than from Communism) and they could not 'do anything but make the worst of both worlds'. Unlike the writers and the statesmen, Orwell recognized that both Communism and Fascism had lost touch with the essentials of democracy; and he spent the thirties, like a weary Jeremiah, warning of the future apocalypse.

While the imperialists declined with the stagnation of the Empire, the intelligentsia took their ideas from Europe and were ashamed of their own nationality. Orwell belonged to both of these classes, and remained isolated within each of them. He understood that the Empire was doomed and welcomed the independence of the colonies, but his contact with imperial and then economic and military reality protected him from 'the emotional shallowness of people who live in a world of ideas'. Unlike the philistine Blimps and the snobbish intelligentsia, Orwell was proud of the common culture of his country and tried to unite patriotism and intelligence in his struggle against totalitarianism.

IV LEAR, TOLSTOY AND THE FOOL (1947)

In his essay on *Gulliver's Travels* (1946), in which he rejects Swift's reactionary ideology but is nevertheless able to admire the terrible intensity of his art, Orwell compares Swift to Tolstoy, 'another disbeliever in the possibility of happiness. In both men you have the same anarchistic outlook covering an authoritarian cast of mind; in both a similar hostility to science, the same impatience with opponents, the same inability to see the importance of any question not interesting to themselves; and in both cases a sort of horror of the actual process of life' (IV.217).

In 'Lear, Tolstoy and the Fool', Orwell analyses Tolstoy's condemnation of *King Lear* in his pamphlet *Shakespeare and Drama*, which was written at the end of his life, in 1903. He suggests that Tolstoy was unable to be critically objective about Shakespeare's art, and that his identification with Lear led to his attack on the play. According to Tolstoy, Shakespeare, far from being a genius, was a less than mediocre author who plagiarized an earlier play and ruined it when he wrote *King Lear*, which was full of moral and aesthetic faults and could be read only with aversion and weariness.

Tolstoy's explanation of how Shakespeare is universally admired despite his immoral ideas and ridiculous language interested Orwell, who was then writing *1984*. The Russian believed that the civilized world was deluded about Shakespeare by a kind of 'mass hypnosis' which only he was able to recognize: 'Goethe pronounced Shakespeare a great poet, whereupon all other critics flocked after him like a troop of parrots, and the general infatuation has lasted ever since.'

After commenting on Tolstoy's extreme bias, insensitivity to the metaphorical (as opposed to the literal) quality of Shakespeare's language, and blindness to Shakespeare's veiled social criticism,

Orwell suggests some important similarities between Lear and the aged Tolstoy. Both were majestic old men 'with flowing white hair and beard, a figure out of Blake's drawings'. This archetype originated with Leonardo's self-portrait and was characteristic of nineteenth-century prophets like Whitman and Darwin. Orwell also draws parallels between Lear's and Tolstoy's spiritual bullying, their gratuitous and misguided renunciation (the basic subject of the play), their exaggerated revulsion from sexuality. Even Tolstoy's final flight from his family accompanied by his only faithful daughter, and his death in a village railway station, seem to have 'a phantom reminiscence of Lear'.

Given these biographical similarities, it was perhaps inevitable that Tolstoy would be angered by Shakespeare's assumptions about Lear's behaviour. For Shakespeare 'points out the results of practising self-denial for selfish reasons', and Tolstoy, 'who tried very hard to make himself into a saint . . . had done no more than exchange one form of egoism for another'. Shakespeare (like Orwell) loved the surface of the earth and the process of life, but Tolstoy renounced the pleasures of earthly life and looked instead to the Kingdom of Heaven.

Orwell is rather cynical about the possibility of secular sainthood and refuses to take Tolstoy at his disciples' valuation. He dislikes the attempt to narrow the range of human consciousness, and does not believe that you can change your basic temperament by experiencing religious conversion: the distinction that really matters, in Lear as in Tolstoy, 'is between having and not having the appetite for power'. Orwell's awareness of the drive for power and domination over others gave him unique insight into Tolstoy's deeper motives for writing about Lear.

V REFLECTIONS ON GANDHI (1949)

Orwell writes in his essay on *King Lear* that 'a sort of doubt always hung round the character of Tolstoy, as round the character of

Gandhi'; and he begins his essay on the Indian nationalist, who shook empires by sheer *spiritual* power, with the aphorism: 'Saints should always be judged guilty until they are proved innocent.'

Like Tolstoy with Lear, Orwell made a partially conscious identification with Gandhi. For, like Orwell, Gandhi 'came of a poor middle-class family, started life rather unfavourably, was probably of unimpressive physical appearance, [but] was *not* afflicted by envy or by the feeling of inferiority'. Orwell first read Gandhi's autobiography (the occasion of the essay) in an Indian newspaper during his Burmese days; and though he associated Gandhi, like the 'pansy-left' whom he attacked in *The Road to Wigan Pier*, with homespun cloth, mysticism and vegetarianism, he was impressed by Gandhi's ethics, honesty and courage.

Orwell criticizes Gandhi for his inhuman tendencies (those who 'aspire to sainthood have never felt much temptation to be human beings') and for his willingness to let his wife or child die rather than give them animal food. The limit of what we will do to remain alive, Orwell believes, 'is well on this side of chicken broth'.

Despite his other-worldly doctrines, Gandhi's real importance was in his political implementation of Thoreau's doctrine of passive resistance – though this technique could only work under a democratic regime like the British Empire. A totalitarian government would have run trains over the first protesters lying down on the tracks, and that would have marked the end of the movement. Though Gandhi was a pacifist, he understood that it was necessary to take sides, and he was a stretcher-bearer on the British side in the Boer War. Though Orwell rejects Tolstoy's and Gandhi's ideal of sainthood, and feels that their basic aims were anti-human and reactionary and that they wanted to escape from love and from the pain of living, Gandhi represents the ideal of patient and obstinate political struggle, untainted by hatred or by greed for power.

VI Benefit of Clergy: Some Notes on Salvador Dali
    (1944)

The relationship of Dali and Orwell is analogous to Huysmans's amusing juxtaposition of the concrete Dickens and the ethereal Gustave Moreau in his novel *Against Nature* (1884). For nothing could be further from the 'disquieting delirium' and the 'potent depravity' of Moreau's painting of the naked and sensual Salome than the 'vulgarity' and virtue of Dickens's 'chaste lovers and his puritanical heroines in their all-concealing draperies'.[2] Through this ironic contrast, Huysmans emphasizes at Dickens's expense the superiority of the imagined to the actual world.

Orwell, who often uses odour as a kind of ethical touchstone, concludes his essay on Gandhi by remarking, 'How clean a smell he has managed to leave behind!'; and he writes that the autobiography of Dali, the personal and moral antithesis of Gandhi, 'is a book that stinks'. For Dali's art represents a direct assault on decency, a quintessential English virtue that Orwell celebrates in his essays on popular culture.

Like Chase's thriller *No Orchids For Miss Blandish* (1939), which glorifies cruelty, sexual perversion and the power instinct and provides 'a day-dream appropriate to a totalitarian age' (III.223), the moral atmosphere of Dali's book, in which he claims to have eaten a dead bat covered with ants, reveals 'the perversion of instinct that has been made possible by the machine age. . . . He is a symptom of the world's illness.' Though Orwell admits that Dali is a hard worker and a brilliant draughtsman, he is not willing to condone the fact that he is 'a disgusting human being' and to extend to him the benefit of clergy that will excuse his moral crimes: his personal cowardice and exhibitionism, his portrayal of sexual perversity and necrophilia.

Orwell uses a witty hyperbole from Dali's autobiography – 'At seven I wanted to be Napoleon. And my ambition has been growing steadily ever since' – to explain his aberrations; and he suggests that, given his egoism and his talent, Dali could only escape into wickedness and achieve fame by shocking and wounding people. But this subjective and moralistic explanation is unsatisfactory for several reasons. Though Orwell writes that Dali's 'dishonest' book is an exaggerated fantasy, he uses everything that Dali says as evidence against him and makes no distinction between dreaming about doing something evil and actually doing it. And he does not grasp the fact that Dali's book is basically Surrealistic fiction and deliberately designed to attack bourgeois values. Orwell naïvely rises to Dali's obvious bait, and unleashes his rather puritanical indignation at the artist who confesses that, when he was five years old, he 'flung another little boy off a suspension bridge'.

Dali is actually writing within a well-established tradition of romantic rebels – from Byron and Baudelaire through the *fin de siècle* decadents (like Huysmans's hero) to Genet and Norman Mailer – who believe that strange sexual habits, bizarre behaviour and a taste for violence stimulate artistic creativity through a kind of individualistic opposition to traditional virtues. Orwell is unable to identify imaginatively with anything so totally alien, and he is so hostile to Dali's *kind* of art that he is incapable of judging it. His attempt to interpret Dali and to relate him to Edwardian painters does not succeed.

If, as Orwell says, there is something wrong with a society in which Dali's 'diseased intelligence' can flourish (while decent drudges like Orwell plod on with little recognition), then the fault must surely lie as much with the society that praises Dali as with Dali himself, who gives society what it wants. Since Dali's appeal is limited and he is not really popular in the way that James Hadley Chase is, Orwell is actually attacking the nameless defenders of Dali, presumably the aristocratic patrons of the arts and *avant-garde* critics who admire his art and do not care about his morals. For such critics there is no need to extend the benefit of clergy. The essential question, which Orwell asks but never answers, is '*why* the *rentiers* and aristocrats should buy his pictures instead of hunting and making love like their grandfathers'. Part of the answer may be, not that Dali is a symptom of the world's illness, but that his art, like Orwell's *1984*, is a meaningful *expression* of that illness.

3 The Ethics of Responsibility:
Burmese Days

> I have tried as best I could to be a man with an
> ethic, and that is what cost me most.
> ALBERT CAMUS

ORWELL IS A LITERARY NONCONFORMIST whose works defy
genres, a writer who is hard to place. His satiric style is like that of
Swift, Butler and Shaw. He has affinities with the school of the great
plain writers – Defoe, Crabbe and Cobbett – the writers of working-
class realism, of human beings in conflict with the class structure.
Dickens, Kipling, Wells, Lawrence and Joyce influenced his early
fiction. Though he was unsympathetic to them, he has some similarities to the Auden–Spender school of the thirties, who, writes
Spender, 'were divided between our literary vocation and an urge
to save the world from Fascism. We were the Divided Generation
of Hamlets who found the world out of joint and failed to set it
right.'[1] But more important than any of these influences and traditions is Orwell's close kinship – in his intense feeling of guilt,
responsibility and commitment – to the French novelists, particularly Malraux and Sartre, who began to write during the inter-
war years, the 'age of guilt'. They have been perceptively analysed by
Victor Brombert, who states that those French writers

> who reached the age of reason around 1930, have suffered from a near-
> pathological guilt complex, and are haunted by what Paul Nizan has
> called the 'social original sin'. . . . The further removed from the scene
> of human anguish, the greater the self-reproach, the more persistent the
> feeling of responsibility. . . . Their message is permanent accusation.
> Silence in the face of social injustice or political tyranny is for them a

shameful *act*, a manner of collaborating with evil. To give society a 'bad conscience' is, according to Sartre, the writer's first duty. . . . The novel of the intellectual has thus been in close contact with all the major events and issues of our time: the problems of democracy, the conflict between the individual and society, between science and religion, the horror of world wars, the threats to justice, the totalitarian menace, the Marxist dream, the Spanish apocalypse of the thirties, the reality of torture and concentration camps . . . the postwar hopes and disillusionments.[2]

Orwell's first novel, the anti-imperialist *Burmese Days* (1934),[3] as well as his later books that attack Fascism, Communism and capitalism, is closely related to the idealism and moral psychology of the French writers, whose guilt is reduced as their commitment is intensified.

Orwell spent five years as a policeman in Burma, and was responsible for the kicking, flogging and torturing of men. The early essay 'A Hanging' (1931), his first treatment of the colonial theme, is a paradigm of his guilt and responsibility. In 'How the Poor Die' Orwell relates how the patients were treated as things rather than as people; in 'Marrakech' he writes that when you walk through a colonial town, 'when you see how the people live, and still more how easily they die, it is always difficult to believe that you are walking among human beings' (1.388); and in *1984* he describes the process of total dehumanization.

The ritualistic requirements of a hanging – from fixed bayonets to a bag over the head of the condemned – help to create that anonymity that is officially desirable during the inhuman circumstances of an execution. The prisoner – brown, silent, passive and puny, with bare feet and torso – is reduced to an elemental level. The warders must constantly feel him to make sure he is there. Both he and his crime are nameless. Because we are unaware of his guilt, we are able to feel the sympathy that is tacitly conveyed by the narrator, who shares the anonymity of the prisoner.

The stray dog who interrupts the procession to the gallows recognizes the humanity of the prisoner, and must also be tied up, straining and whimpering as if in protest. When the prisoner steps around the puddle he verifies his existence by an act of conscious will, and the narrator uses this trivial incident to reveal the theme of his essay: 'He was alive just as we were alive' (1.45).

Another prisoner acts as the hangman to diminish official responsibility; and the dog's whine, which echoes the prisoner's prayer, acts as a sonant conscience. The Superintendent's remark that the dead man is 'all right' is both ironic and, in an awful sense, true. The whole incident has taken eight minutes and nothing is left of the man but his footprints on the wet earth. The need to relieve the unbearable tension through laughter at the gruesome anecdotes of hangings merely emphasizes the earlier excision of emotion, both in the executioners and in the prisoner. The steady prayer in his last moments contrasts to his involuntary pissing when he hears that his appeal has been denied. The final irony is that only a meaningless death – for even the essay has not invested it with significance – can bring the English and the natives together. The system is totally corrupt and inhuman.

Orwell saw the dirty work of Empire at close quarters and 'the horribly ugly, degrading scenes which offend one's eyes all the time in the starved countries of the East', where an Indian coolie's leg is often thinner than an Englishman's arm (II.217). By the end of five years, writes Orwell, 'I hated the imperialism I was serving with a bitterness which I probably cannot make clear . . . it is not possible to be a part of such a system without recognizing it as an unjustifiable tyranny. . . . I was conscious of an immense weight of guilt that I had got to expiate.'[4]

Orwell managed to relieve this intense guilt in two ways. He resigned his position, and to expiate his political sin submerged himself among the oppressed poor of Paris and London and took their side against the tyrants by becoming one of them. For obvious reasons of caste and race this kind of masochistic submergence was impossible in Asia, but for Orwell the European working classes 'were the symbolic victims of injustice, playing the same part in England as the Burmese played in Burma'.[5] Orwell also relieved his guilt through creative exorcism (as he did in 'Such, Such'), for he writes that 'the landscapes of Burma, which, when I was among them, so appalled me as to assume the qualities of a nightmare, afterwards stayed so hauntingly in my mind that I was obliged to write a novel about them to get rid of them'.[6] This accounts for the novel's passionate and didactic quality.

The central political principle in *Burmese Days* derives from Montesquieu, who wrote in *The Spirit of the Laws* (1748), 'If a democratic republic subdues a nation in order to govern them as subjects, it exposes its own liberty.' The truth of this principle is illustrated by the Burmese judge U Po Kyin, who is clearly modelled on the physical characteristics of the Malay chief Doramin in Conrad's *Lord Jim* (1900). Both Orientals are lavishly dressed, enormously fat, need assistance to rise from their chairs, and habitually confer with their wives.[7] U Po is the *primum mobile* of all events in the novel, an underling who has the most actual power in the English outpost of progress and who, through devious machinations, controls even his rulers. He slanders the Deputy Commissioner Macgregor, ruins the Indian Dr Veraswami, incites a rebellion in which two men are killed, and drives the hero, Flory, to suicide. A fair sample of the Burmese magistrate, U Po has advanced himself by thievery, bribery, blackmail and betrayal, and his corrupt career is a serious criticism of both the English rule that permits his success and his English superiors who so disastrously misjudge his character.

The object of U Po's intrigues, and the Nirvana for which he longs, is the English Club, the last fortress of white insularity. Orwell's ironic juxtaposition of native and English social scenes reveals the sleazy Club just after U Po has made his fabulous wish. Besides Flory, the English colony consists of the bigoted and malicious Ellis, the drunken and lecherous Lackersteen, his scheming and snobbish wife, the bloodthirsty and stupid Westfield, the boring and pompous Macgregor, the innocent and inoffensive Maxwell and, later on, the arrogant and cruel Verrall.[8] There are no redeeming characters in Orwell's negative novel, only the 'dull boozing witless porkers' who exploit the country and observe the five beatitudes of the *pukka sahib*:

Keeping up our prestige,
The firm hand (without the velvet glove),
We white men must hang together,
Give them an inch and they'll take an ell, and
Esprit de Corps.

They strive to impose the 'Pox Britannica' which, prophesies Flory, will eventually wreck 'the whole Burmese national culture. We're not civilizing them, we're only rubbing our dirt on to them.'

Orwell writes in his essay on Kipling that 'Civilised men do not readily move away from the centres of civilisation'; and the philistine values of the Club are essentially the values of Kipling, whose view of life, Orwell states, cannot 'be accepted or even forgiven by any civilised person. . . . Kipling *is* a jingo imperialist, he *is* morally insensitive and aesthetically disgusting' (II.184,192). Kipling, the first major English writer to deal extensively and seriously with the British colonies, was the most popular and influential author of his age, and his ideas about colonialism were the ones that overwhelmingly prevailed until the 1920s and well beyond.[9]

It was Kipling's image of India that inspired the ideological opposition in the novels of Empire that followed in the genre he had created. In *A Passage to India, Burmese Days, Mister Johnson* and *The Heart of the Matter*, the English officials who express Kipling's ideals and values are portrayed in a negative light; and what was serious doctrine for Kipling becomes ironic in the novels of Forster, Orwell, Cary and Greene, who record the decline of British imperialism just as Kipling had celebrated its greatness.

Though Orwell writes that the English in India 'could not have maintained themselves in power for a single week, if the normal Anglo-Indian outlook had been that of, say, E. M. Forster' (II.187), *Burmese Days* was strongly influenced by *A Passage to India*, which was published in 1924 when Orwell was serving in Burma. Both novels concern an Englishman's friendship with an Indian doctor, and a girl who goes out to the colonies, gets engaged and then breaks it off. Both use the Club scenes to reveal a cross-section of colonial society, and both measure the personality and value of the characters by their racial attitudes. The themes of lack of understanding and the difficulties of friendship between English and natives, the physical deterioration and spiritual corruption of the whites in the tropics, are sounded by Forster and echo through Orwell's novel. But *Burmese Days* is a far more pessimistic book than *A Passage to India*, because official failures are not redeemed by successful personal relations. There are no characters, like Fielding and Mrs Moore, who are able to prevail against the overwhelming cruelty of the English and maintain a civilized standard of behaviour.

Fielding is the exception to the rule that 'The English always stick together!', for he defends Aziz against the uniform opposition of the entire Club, and cuts himself off from the English community by staking his reputation and integrity on his friend's innocence. He has a strong feeling of common humanity, and strives for a union of perfect equality with people of different races. Unlike all the other Englishmen, he rejects the sahib's role, and is not corrupted by officialism or by life in the tropics.

The moral conflicts of *A Passage to India* are presented in Flory's everlasting argument with his friend Dr Veraswami, a loyal British subject who always defends imperialism and who also aspires to Club membership for prestige and as protection against his enemies. Flory reveals his moral weakness first by refusing to support his friend's nomination and then by allowing himself to be coerced into signing a statement against native members. Like Orwell, Flory hates to see the English humiliating the Asians, and is ashamed of the imperialistic exploitation and class distinctions. But he recognizes, in an ironic paraphrase of Kipling, that 'even friendship can hardly exist when every white man is a cog in the wheels of despotism'.

This connection between political oppression and private guilt has been acutely described by Nietzsche, who writes that 'Political superiority without any real human superiority is most harmful. One must seek to make amends for political superiority. To be *ashamed* of one's power.'[10] Flory, of course, is ashamed, but his failure to come to terms with the intolerable colonial situation is symbolized by his hideous birthmark – as much a sign of guilt, a mark of Cain, as an indication of his isolation and alienation. He is unable to mediate between the three worlds of Burma: the English, the 'native' and the natural world of the jungle.

The second part of the novel begins with the arrival of the shallow and selfish Elizabeth Lackersteen, whom Flory sees as the only salvation from his Burmese misery. But they fail to understand each other, and Flory's efforts to introduce Elizabeth to the Burmese world of dance-plays and market-places, to make her appreciate and admire the country as he does, result only in insulting his Oriental friends and revolting Elizabeth, who prefers English society. Nevertheless, their parabolic courtship progresses in a series of physical adventures: they meet as Flory rescues Elizabeth from a water buffalo, and decide to marry first after shooting a leopard and again after Flory's heroic swim to rescue the besieged Club members, when the rioting Burmese all want to 'get into' the Club.

Their only communion occurs during the central hunting episode, when Flory teaches Elizabeth to shoot and she kills the beautiful jade pigeons that Flory had previously observed while peacefully performing a Thoreau-like baptism in the lonely jungle, where he sought refuge and relief from his penitential solitude and guilt. When the limp and warm iridescent fowl is placed in Elizabeth's hand, her desire for Flory is awakened, and the connection between sexual passion and destructive violence (foreshadowing Flory's suicide) is subtly revealed. When Flory shoots a male leopard, his gift of the skin silently seals their troth. Later on, the ruined leopard skin, like Flory's facial skin, is both a cause and a symbol of Elizabeth's disaffection.

Orwell is concerned with how his characters face responsibility, and Flory's inability to meet responsibility under the pressure of an overwhelming guilt is shown in his relationships with Dr Veraswami, whom he proposes to the Club only when it is too late; and with his Burmese mistress, May Hla, whom he abandons and then bribes after a mutually destructive liaison, and who decays in a brothel after exposing him before Elizabeth and the English community;[11] and finally with Elizabeth herself, whom he can neither enlighten nor engage. His suicide, a violent yet appropriate gesture of physical courage and moral cowardice, is his terrible protest against these failures. Flory's suicide is a way of concluding the novel, but it is an essentially weak device that resolves neither the themes of the book nor the problems inherent in the colonial experience.

Orwell states that 'When a subject population rises in revolt you have got to suppress it, and you can only do so by methods which make nonsense of any claim for the superiority of western civilization. In order to rule over barbarians you have got to become a barbarian yourself' (I.235). This emphasizes the personal and political themes of *Burmese Days* that are fused, and again related to death, in Orwell's famous essay 'Shooting an Elephant', written two years later in 1936.

Lionel Trilling suggests the complexity of emotion in this essay, which is representative of Orwell's best style and technique: 'He has spoken with singular honesty of the ambiguousness of his attitude in the imperialist situation. He disliked authority and the manner of its use, and he sympathized with the natives; yet at the same time he saw the need for authority and he used it, and he was often exasperated by the natives.'[12] The striking opening sentence emphasizes the paradox of hatred and importance, and expresses political hostility in terms of human vulnerability: 'In Moulmein, in Lower Burma, I was hated by large numbers of people – the only time in my life that I have been important enough for this to happen to me.' This hatred, expressed in the chromatic detail of Burmese spitting red betel juice on white English dresses and in the irony of Buddhist priests jeering instead of praying, shows a tension quite different from Orwell's statement that, when he was there, 'nationalist feelings in Burma were not very marked, and relations between the English and the Burmese were not particularly bad' (III.403). Torn between hatred of colonialism and hatred of the colonized, Orwell uses a personal experience to illustrate a political truth.

As a policeman, Orwell is summoned to help when an elephant in heat breaks loose from chains and trainer and wreaks violence on the Burmese community. Orwell's entrance into the 'labyrinth of squalid bamboo huts' to slay the huge beast that has claimed human victims ironically suggests the mythic overtones of Theseus and the Minotaur. He finds the dead coolie, and describes him in vivid and precise detail that contrasts the martyred pose with the meaningless death, the grin with the torture: he was 'lying on his belly with arms crucified and head sharply twisted to one side. His face was coated with mud, the eyes wide open, the teeth bared and grinning with an expression of unendurable agony.'

Orwell introduces the central theatrical metaphor of appearance and reality, mask and spectacle, when he marches toward the elephant 'looking and feeling a fool'. He surrenders reason to emotion, will to passivity, as the Eastern masses quietly dominate the Western 'leader'. He realizes that political oppression is self-destructive when he perceives the major theme of the essay: 'When the white man turns tyrant it is his own freedom that he destroys.'

At this point the elephant is first introduced, and his 'preoccupied grandmotherly air' makes him attractive and humanized. Yet he is still dangerous: 'If anything went wrong those two thousand Burmans would see me pursued, caught, trampled on and reduced to a grinning corpse like that Indian up the hill. And if that happened it was quite probable that some of them would laugh. That would never do.' The third ironic 'that' has a deliberately indefinite antecedent (corpse or laugh) which subtly links Orwell with the Asians in their common desire to 'save face'.

The death of the elephant is described with a lively compassion that reinforces its 'grandmotherly air': 'A mysterious, terrible change had come over the elephant. . . . He looked suddenly stricken, shrunken, immensely old. . . . But in falling he seemed for a moment to rise, for as his hind legs collapsed beneath him, he seemed to tower upwards like a huge rock toppling, his trunk reaching skywards like a tree.' The final sentence suggests an enormous natural disaster – a landslide or an earthquake. The effect that Orwell achieves, of vividness, intensity, pain and penetration, is similar to Hemingway's description of the wounded lion in 'The

Short Happy Life of Francis Macomber', for Orwell sympathizes with the wounded, innocent elephant just as Hemingway identifies with the powerful, charging lion: the solid bullet 'bit his flank and ripped in sudden hot scalding nausea through his stomach. . . . Then it crashed again and he felt the blow as it hit his lower ribs and ripped on through, blood sudden hot and frothy in his mouth.'[13]

The elephant, Orwell writes, 'was dying, very slowly and in great agony, but in some world remote from me. . . . It seemed dreadful to see the great beast lying there, powerless to move and yet powerless to die.' The echo of Arnold's 'Wandering between two worlds, one dead,/The other powerless to be born' stresses the symbolic connection between the dying elephant and the dying Empire. And this is, of course, related to the two major themes: that injustice leads to political self-destruction, and that 'the British Empire is dying'.

In 'England Your England', Orwell suggests an important reason why the death of Empire is inherent in its 'social injustice' and 'political tyranny': by 1920, two years before he went out to Burma, 'nearly every inch of the colonial empire was in the grip of Whitehall. Well-meaning, overcivilised men, in dark suits and black felt hats, with neatly rolled umbrellas crooked over the left forearm, were imposing their constipated view of life on Malaya and Nigeria, Mombasa and Mandalay' (II.73). Through the *personae* of Flory and the shooter of elephants, Orwell exposes the radical limitations not only of the *sahibs* ruling Burma, but also of the rigid though all-encompassing imperialistic ideology. And when he assumed the guise of an honorary proletarian, rejected dark suits, felt hats and rolled umbrellas, and visited the slums of London and Wigan, he discovered that the overcivilized bureaucrats who ran the colonies also imposed their constipated and capitalistic views on the working classes, whose values and way of life were foreign to their rulers and who were dominated with the same lack of understanding as the Burmese.

4   The Honorary Proletarian: Orwell and Poverty

> Sir, all the arguments which are brought to represent poverty as no evil, shew it to be evidently a great evil.
>
> SAMUEL JOHNSON

I

JUST AFTER HE RETURNED from Burma, in 1928–29, Orwell lived in a working-class quarter of Paris and worked as a dishwasher, 'a slave's slave'. In *Down and Out in Paris and London* Orwell suggests that both Asian and European workers suffer similar injustices, though he does not develop this idea until *The Road to Wigan Pier*, whose title may have been suggested by 'The Road to Mandalay'. When Orwell writes of the English tramp Paddy, for example, 'Seeing him walk, you felt instinctively that he would sooner take a blow than give one,'[1] it is clear that this 'instinctive' feeling grew directly out of his experiences in Burma where he did the dirty work of Empire, was responsible for 'the scarred buttocks of the men who had been flogged with bamboos' (I.236) and saw 'louts fresh from school kicking grey-haired servants'.[2] This made him burn with hatred of his countrymen and of himself. Similarly, the equation of exploitation with luxury in his analysis of the upper-class attitude toward the poor: 'since evidently you must sweat to pay for our trips to Italy, sweat and be damned to you',[3] again recalls the colonial parallel: 'As the world is now constituted, we are all standing on the backs of half-starved coolies.'[4]

'We all live in terror of poverty' (III.189), writes Orwell, and its psychological and social effects are one of his dominant themes.

Though almost all of his books treat this question in a significant way (the exploited natives in *Burmese Days*, the plight of the common soldier in *Homage to Catalonia* and of the dehumanized proles in *1984*), Orwell's four books of the depressed mid-thirties – *Down and Out in Paris and London* (1933), *A Clergyman's Daughter* (1935), *Keep the Aspidistra Flying* (1936) and *The Road to Wigan Pier* (1937) – are completely devoted to the exploration of this theme. Works like *New Grub Street*, *The Spoils of Poynton*, *Nostromo*, *Howards End* and *Major Barbara* all deal, in their different ways, with the corruption of capitalistic society; Orwell's books consider the working classes who are exploited by this corrupt society.

One of Orwell's main ideas can be found in Shaw's Preface to *Major Barbara* (1907): 'The greatest of evils and the worst of crimes is poverty.' For Shaw, a half-century before Orwell, 'was drawn into the Socialist revival of the early eighties, among Englishmen intensely serious and burning with indignation at the very real and very fundamental evils that affected all the world'.[5] But Orwell's desire to experience these evils directly and personally (as he had done in Burma), to break out of the emotionally shallow and sheltered state of the middle classes and make contact with physical reality, 'to look down at the roots on which his existence is founded',[6] is quite different from the Victorian philanthropy of Dickens and Shaw. His need to share the poverty and hardship, which does not actually help the poor in the way that his books do (though it may have enabled him to write better books), relates him more closely to 'committed' writers like Malraux and Sartre. In the autobiographical ninth chapter of *Wigan Pier*, Orwell explains his motives and relates how the overpowering guilt that resulted from his years as a policeman in Burma forced him to seek expiation among the down-and-outs of Paris and London. Though Orwell knows he can belong to this world only 'temporarily', he is desperate to be accepted, for only then can he begin to shed his guilt:

> I wanted to submerge myself, to get right down among the oppressed, to be one of them and on their side against their tyrants. . . . Therefore

my mind turned immediately towards the extreme cases, the social outcasts: tramps, beggars, criminals, prostitutes. . . . I could go among these
people, see what their lives were like and feel myself temporarily part of
their world. Once I had been among them and accepted by them, I should
have touched bottom and – this is what I felt: I was aware even then it
was irrational – part of my guilt would drop from me. . . . And down
there in the squalid and, as a matter of fact, horribly boring sub-world of
the tramp I had a feeling of release, of adventure, which seems absurd
when I look back, but which was sufficiently vivid at the time.[7]

Many of Orwell's most characteristic ideas about responsibility are
stated in this passage: the desire to have immediate and actual
experience, to see things from the inside rather than from a purely
theoretical viewpoint; to fight on the side of the oppressed and to
agonize over their sufferings; to extinguish, among out-castes, the
sense of social class; to feel the pleasurable relief, the anxiety and
guilt-annihilating euphoria of going to the dogs and knowing you
can stand it; to undergo the excitement of a *sortie* to the lower depths.

Books like Johnson's *Life of Savage*, Zola's *Germinal*, Crane's
Maggie, Gorki's *The Lower Depths*, Davies's *Autobiography of a Super
Tramp* and Jack London's *The Road*, which had vividly portrayed
the outcasts at the extreme fringe of society, were pioneering works
of intensely personal social protest. But the most immediate influence on *Down and Out* was London's *The People of the Abyss*
(1903). In his Preface, London likened himself to an explorer of the
underworld and wrote, 'What I wish to do, is to go down into the
East End and see things for myself. I wish to know how these people
are living there, and why they are living there, and what they are
living for. In short, I am going to live there myself.'[8] While London
seeks the same direct and documentary experience as Orwell did,
he lacks Orwell's emotional involvement and explores the strange
slums of the East End as if they were the Arctic tundra.

In his summary chapter of the Paris section of *Down and Out*,
Orwell compares the slavery and suffering of a *plongeur* to that of a
coal miner; and the most striking example of the continuity of
Orwell's books in this period is the similarity of the descriptions of
the infernal *plongeur*'s cellar and the hellish mine in Wigan:

[I came] into a narrow passage, deep underground, and so low that I had to stoop in places. It was stifling hot and very dark, with only dim yellow bulbs several yards apart. There seemed to be miles of dark labyrinthine passages – actually, I suppose, a few hundred yards in all – that reminded one queerly of the lower decks of a liner; there were the same heat and cramped space and warm reek of food, and a humming, whirring noise. . . . It was too low for me to stand quite upright, and the temperature was perhaps 110 degrees Fahrenheit. . . . Scullions, naked to the waist, were stoking the fires. (*Down and Out*)

Most of the things one imagines in hell are there – heat, noise, confusion, darkness, foul air, and above all, unbearably cramped space. . . . You can never forget . . . the line of bowed, [naked] kneeling figures, sooty black all over, driving their huge shovels under the coal with stupendous force and speed. (*Wigan Pier*)

The theme of class exploitation is dramatized most vividly in *Down and Out* amidst the luxury and squalor of the grand hotel where the splendid customers sit just a few feet away from the disgusting filth of the kitchen workers. The only connection between these two worlds is the food prepared by one for the other, which often contains the cook's spit and the waiter's hair grease. From this fact Orwell posits a wonderfully ironic economic law: 'The more one pays for food, the more sweat and spittle one is obliged to eat with it.'

One of the larger ironies of the book is that Orwell fled this unjust social hierarchy only to find, among the down-and-out, an even more elaborate and rigidly military caste system. The staff of the hotel descended from the exalted heights of the *patron* and manager, through the *maître d'hôtel*, head cook, *chef du personnel*, other cooks and waiters, to laundresses, apprentice waiters and finally *plongeurs*, who aspired to become lavatory attendants and had only chambermaids and *cafetiers* below them. And a sharp distinction also existed between those London beggars 'who merely cadge and those who attempt to give some value for money'.

Perhaps the most interesting aspect of the book, apart from the revelation of Orwell's character, is his description of the psychology of poverty, as he discovered it in the hotels, hospitals, pawnshops

and parks of the mean and degenerate Paris, and in his 'very narrow
street – a ravine of tall, leprous houses, lurching towards one another
in queer attitudes, as though they had all been frozen in the act of
collapse', whose decrepit and sinister aspect suggests the city of Zola
and of Baudelaire's 'Tableaux Parisiens'.

Orwell seemed happier as a *plongeur* than as an English tramp,
perhaps because it was easier to be *déclassé* outside his own country,
and because he was fresher and the Parisian life had an exotic tinge
despite the patina of antique filth. He speaks of the eccentric freedom from the normal and the decent, the mindless acceptance when
you reach destitution after anticipating it for so long, the animal
contentment of the simple rhythm of work and sleep. But in the
long run, of course, the degrading human effects are disastrous.
Hunger reduces men to a spineless, brainless condition and mal-
nutrition destroys their manhood, while extreme poverty cuts men
off from contact with women: 'The evil of poverty is not so much
that it makes a man suffer as that it rots him physically and spiritually.'

Orwell's suggestions for the alleviation of poverty are both
pragmatic and politic, and he hopes to improve conditions by
clarifying common misconceptions in the light of first-hand
experience: 'You thought it would be quite simple; it is extraordinarily complicated. You thought it would be terrible; it is
merely squalid and boring.' Like Dickens, who tried to persuade his
middle-class audience that the poor were not evil and were not to be
blamed for their poverty, Orwell explodes a number of common
prejudices by explaining them. Educated people fear workers because
they do not understand them and despise beggars because they fail to
earn a decent living. (That 'money has become the grand test of
virtue'[9] is a major theme of *Keep the Aspidistra Flying*.) Tramps tramp
because they are compelled by law to do so; they are too docile to
be dangerous and too destitute to be drunk. Orwell, middle-class by
birth and working-class by experience, contrasts the two classes in
order to reveal how hatred and fear force them into opposition.

Orwell not only criticizes the harsh and unfair laws governing
tramps, but also suggests making the casual wards more comfortable

and finding suitable employment for the men, possibly through small farms attached to the workhouses. But all these are minor palliatives; the solution implicit in the book, though not stated until *Wigan Pier*, is Socialism; and it was Orwell's experience among the poor and outcast in Paris and London that made him aware of the need for that radical change which involves not only a more equitable distribution of wealth, but also a sincere concern for the welfare of impoverished people:

> If one judges capitalism by what it has actually achieved – the horrors of the Industrial Revolution, the destruction of one culture after another, the piling-up of millions of human beings in hideous ant-heaps of cities, and, above all, the enslavement of the coloured races – it is difficult to feel that in itself it is superior to feudalism.[10]

II

Both *A Clergyman's Daughter* and *Keep the Aspidistra Flying* concern the unsuccessful attempt to escape from the boredom and triviality of a middle-class existence. Both Dorothy and Gordon, after experiences with meanness and poverty similar to those Orwell described in *Down and Out*, return to the economic security of their former lives and (somewhat unconvincingly) reaffirm its values: religious, for Dorothy; familial, for Gordon. The core of *A Clergyman's Daughter*, chapters II on hop-picking and III on tramps in Trafalgar Square, is based on Orwell's forays among the poor that began as early as 1927 and continued throughout the next decade. He went hop-picking in September 1931 and many parts of his early essay about this (and about his arrest, described in 'Clink', 1932) are interpolated into the novel.[11] Chapters I and v, which concern a degrading and pinch-penny life of shabby-gentility, as seen both before and after a direct confrontation with real poverty, take place in a rectory of a small East Anglian town, where Orwell lived in the early 1930s and where he wrote the novel.

Orwell raises the central critical questions about the novel in his rather harsh comments about his weakest book. He was ashamed of the novel, called it 'bollox' and 'tripe' and, when he finished it in late 1934, wrote to his agent: 'I am not at all pleased with it. It was a good idea, but I am afraid I have made a muck of it – however, it is as good as I can do for the present. There are bits of it that I don't dislike, but I am afraid it is very disconnected as a whole, and rather unreal' (I.141). This severe but honest letter identifies the two main faults of the novel: its weak structure and unconvincing plot. Orwell was undoubtedly thinking of this book when he criticized the style of his early work in his retrospective 'Why I Write': 'Looking back through my work, I see that it is invariably where I lacked a *political* purpose that I wrote lifeless books and was betrayed into purple passages, sentences without meaning, decorative adjectives and humbug generally' (I.7).[12]

Though a political or polemical purpose might have inspired a greater seriousness and dedication, the real failure of *A Clergyman's Daughter* is Orwell's inability to find the correct form to embrace his experience and embody his ideas. As he realized, the novel's divergent and disconnected episodes – in the rectory, with hop-pickers and tramps, and at the school – are essentially autobiographical and linked by the weakest transitions. Dorothy is transported into the squalid and boring world of the tramp by an unexplained loss of memory (Orwell's use of psychology is extremely weak), and he omits the most potentially interesting part of the book by ignoring what happened to the heroine during the first eight days between Suffolk and London. Then her memory, stimulated by her friend's arrest and the newspaper headlines, returns quite suddenly. She is unexpectedly rescued from poverty and despair, first by her cousin's sleuth-like butler, and then by the appearance of Warburton, her sometime admirer, whose proposal she rejects on the grounds of sexual frigidity, despite his accurate predictions of her dreary and desolate future.[13]

Dorothy has a hare-like timidity which, combined with her spinsterish, frigid and masochistic personality (she inflicts medieval mortifications on herself for petty offences), makes her a perfect victim. Though she does not deserve cruel treatment at the hands of her father, Mrs Creevy and even Warburton (the tramps treat her well), she certainly needs their punishment to relieve the intense guilt she shares with her creator. The repressive and sterile milieu of the rectory recalls Lawrence's 'Daughters of the Vicar' (1911), of which Orwell writes: 'Probably Lawrence had watched, somewhere or other, the underfed, downtrodden, organ-playing daughter of a clergyman wearing out her youth, and had a sudden vision of her escaping into the warmer world of the working class' (IV.33).[14] But the working class does not provide the comfort and refuge for Dorothy that it did for Orwell. During the cold horrors of the Square she asks, 'How can you stand it? How can you go on like this, night after night, year after year?'

Dorothy's only successful, though very ephemeral, escape is into nature-worship. During her exhausting parish visits, she stops to breathe the scent of childhood happiness and to experience that 'mystical joy in the beauty of the earth', only to discover 'that she was kissing the frond of the fennel that was still against her face', a sad sexual substitute. This scene is contrasted to her dreary walks in the school holidays through 'the mean suburban roads, the damp, miry paths through the woods, the naked trees, the sodden moss and great spongy fungi, [that] afflicted her with a deadly melancholy' and that are the rural equivalent of the depressing labyrinthine London landscape in which she lives.

Like that of *Keep the Aspidistra Flying*, the structure of *A Clergyman's Daughter* is circular, and the mood is set in the first sentence of the novel, which is similar to the opening of Kafka's 'The Metamorphosis' (1916):

> As Gregor Samsa awoke one morning from uneasy dreams he found himself transformed in his bed into a gigantic insect.

> Dorothy, wrenched from the depths of some complex, troubling dream, awoke with a start and lay on her back looking into the darkness in extreme exhaustion.

Dorothy's disturbing dream reveals her need to repress subconscious fears and foreshadows the amnesia that allows her to escape by metamorphosis into an irresponsible tramp, a strange relief after the agonies of humiliating poverty. What Dorothy tries to repress is the hatred of her father, who is responsible for her three greatest anxieties: lack of money, loss of faith and sexual frigidity. Orwell rather superficially attributes Dorothy's sexual coldness, a characteristic of all his heroines, to 'certain dreadful scenes between her father and her mother' that she had witnessed at nine years old and that 'had left a deep, secret wound in her mind'. Dorothy's three anxieties converge in the Square scene when the recurrent dreams 'grow more monstrous, troubling and undreamlike' as Mr Tallboys (who combines the profession and nostalgia for happier days of her father with the immorality of Warburton) creates an image of earthly Hell in a Baudelairean metaphor of blasphemy and squalor:

> He has afflicted us with dirt and cold, with hunger and solitude, with the pox and the itch, with the headlouse and the crablouse. . . . Our pleasure is . . . the embrace of toothless hags. Our destiny is the pauper's grave twenty-five deep in deal coffins, the kip-house of the underground.

As the defrocked priest recites the Lord's Prayer backwards, Dorothy is forced back into the Kafkaesque world of atavistic guilt and fear:

> He tears the consecrated bread across. The blood runs out of it. . . . Monstrous winged shapes of Demons and Archdemons are dimly visible, moving to and fro. Something, beak or claw, closes upon Dorothy's shoulder.

This phantasmagoric nightmare symbolizes, in religious imagery, Dorothy's 'terrifying and repulsive' fears of sexual assault, for when Warburton attacked her 'outrageously, even brutally . . . she struggled in his arms, violently and for a moment helplessly'.

Though this Square scene was the only part of the novel Orwell was 'pleased with' (1.150), Woodcock calls it 'the weakest part of the novel, because Orwell is using a self-conscious literary device in an attempt to dismiss the fact that at this point he is rather clumsily grafting his own adventures and observations in the London tramp world on to Dorothy's story'.[15] But it is only in this scene, however clumsy, that the themes of the novel fuse into a coherent whole.

Dorothy's conflicts about sexuality and religion lead to her decision at the end of the novel to reject marriage with Warburton, and to return to her father and (at least) the external manifestations of religion: 'There was, she saw clearly, no possible substitute for faith. . . . Either life on earth is a preparation for something greater and more lasting, or it is meaningless, dark and dreadful.'

Orwell, like Dorothy, was ambivalent about religion. He had the desire to believe but not the power to do so. He rejected the doctrine of the Church but felt that it had 'something of decency, of spiritual comeliness – that is not easily found in the world outside', that it is 'better to follow in the ancient ways, than to drift in rootless freedom'.[16] In 'England Your England' he admires 'the old maids biking to Holy Communion through the mists of the autumn mornings, [who] are . . . *characteristic* fragments of the English scene' (II.57); but in the novel Dorothy rides through the gloomy mist and sodden grass to a church that 'loomed dimly, like a leaden sphinx, its single bell tolling funereally'. The description of the large, cold, empty church 'with a scent of candle-wax and ancient dust' is like George Bowling's ambivalent description of the church in Lower Binfield, satiric yet nostalgic:

> You know the smell churches have, a peculiar, dank, dusty, decaying, sweetish sort of smell. There's a touch of candlegrease in it, and perhaps a whiff of incense and a suspicion of mice . . . but predominantly it's that sweet, dusty, musty smell that's like the smell of death and life mixed up together. It's powdered corpses, really.[17]

For Orwell, as for Dorothy and Bowling, religion is associated with the fixed and familiar order of the pre-war period, when it was still possible to have a satisfying and coherent world view, and he misses the sense of holiness that has disappeared from contemporary life. Orwell writes of the Rector, an entirely unsympathetic character, 'He ought never to have been born into the modern world; its whole atmosphere disgusted and infuriated him. A couple of centuries earlier, a happy pluralist writing poems . . . he would have been perfectly at home.' Yet in this respect he is not so different from Orwell himself, who wrote in 1936, the year after the novel:

A happy vicar I might have been
Two hundred years ago,
To preach upon eternal doom
And watch my walnuts grow;

But born, alas, in evil time,
I missed that pleasant haven ... (1.4)

The unsatisfactory and disappointing conclusion of the novel suggests that religion is not Orwell's central concern, for the final conflict between faith and atheism simply disappears into a bland, deistic, social Christianity: 'Faith and no faith *are very much the same* provided that one is doing what is customary, useful and acceptable' (italics mine). Orwell's rather inappropriate quotation of Mark ix, 24, 'Lord, I believe, help Thou my unbelief' and the conclusion with Dorothy's pious concentration on the stiffening gluepot, recall E. M. Forster's tougher and more consistent credo, 'What I Believe':

> I do not believe in Belief. ... Faith, to my mind, is a stiffening process, a sort of mental starch, which ought to be applied as sparingly as possible. I dislike the stuff. ... My motto is: 'Lord, I disbelieve – help thou my unbelief.'[18]

Forster's ironic variation of the Gospel conveys the sense of Orwell's nostalgic Anglicanism as well as of his own.

Although *A Clergyman's Daughter* fails as a novel, its parts, considered separately, are individually successful. Orwell could have solved the problem of how to write about his personal experience by using most of it in non-fictional books, for he is never comfortable or convincing in the *persona* of Dorothy. In a 1948 letter he confesses his inability to assimilate and transform this personal experience into fiction: 'One difficulty I have never solved is that one has masses of experience which one passionately wants to write about ... and no way of using them up except by disguising them as a novel' (IV.422). In this novel, the experience is 'disguised 'too transparently and is reported rather than rendered. The chapters on tramping could have been incorporated into *Down and Out* and the section on teaching made into an autobiographical essay that would complement 'Such, Such', while the religious chapters would have been better as a unified and concentrated short story. Both Dorothy and Gordon Comstock have an unattractive streak of self-pity that disappears in *Down and Out* and *The Road to Wigan Pier*. These books are superior to the early novels, not merely because they have a political purpose, but because in these works Orwell creates a successful *persona* that interprets experience in a direct and meaningful way.

III

Keep the Aspidistra Flying, like *Down and Out*, has a balanced structure. Paris and London, Boris and Paddy, the good and bad hotels, the castes of *plongeurs* and beggars, the summaries with practical suggestions at the end of each half, are contrasted in the earlier book. The same kind of technique is also used in the novel, where it emphasizes the circular pattern of the book (the return to the advertising office) as well as the two phases of Gordon's life: before and after the drunken spree. McKechnie's and Cheeseman's bookshops; Mrs Wisbeach's and Mrs Meakin's rooms; the friendship of Flaxman and Ravelston; the love of his sister Julia and his girl Rosemary;[19] and the two sexual encounters with Rosemary, are ironically contrasted. For the worse job and the dingier room seem 'better' to Gordon; though he is closer to Ravelston and Rosemary, he finds it easier to accept help from Flaxman and Julia; and the lyrical seduction scene is a failure while the squalid one is all too successful.

Several other structural motifs emphasize Gordon's resolution to return to the respectable middle-class moneyed world, symbolized by the indestructible aspidistra and the New Albion advertising company. At the end of the novel, Gordon and Rosemary have their wedding feast at the modest Soho restaurant that Ravelston had previously suggested they go to, instead of the disastrously expensive Modigliani's (which parallels the fashionable country hotel); they live in a flat with a view of Paddington, from where they had left on their country outing; Gordon sprouts grey hairs to match Rosemary's (a weak symbol of his 'mature' acceptance of life) and she pulls hers out for the wedding ceremony; and as a comfortably employed writer and prospective father, he relinquishes his apocalyptic wish and no longer craves the destruction of London by bombs.

Despite Orwell's evident care with the form of the novel, the mechanical plot has some serious weaknesses. The chance meeting with Rosemary in the open-air market seems too coincidental; and the mystery of how the previously unacquainted Flaxman and Ravelston, Rosemary and Julia ever got together to 'save' Gordon is never explained. Ravelston's inability to resist the 'abominable adventure' with the whores seems incredible; and, worst of all, Rosemary becomes pregnant after her first sexual encounter, in the archaic tradition of the Victorian novel.

Nor is Orwell in full control of his style in this novel, which is repetitive to the point of boredom and exasperation ('Money, money, always money!') and liberally sprinkled with poetic allusions (Gordon is, or was, a poet) which are rather forced and banal:

> Novels fresh from the press – still unravished brides, pining for the paper-knife to deflower them – and review copies, like youthful widows, blooming still though virgin no longer, and here and there, in sets of half a dozen, those pathetic spinster-things, 'remainders', still guarding hopefully their long preserv'd virginity.[20]

Besides quotations in this passage from Keats and Marvell, there are ineffectual allusions to the Bible, Virgil, Chaucer, Villon, Wyatt, Peele, Shakespeare, Milton, Mandeville, Blake, Baudelaire, Francis Thompson and D. H. Lawrence, and Orwell's laborious use of poetic allusion is another example of his difficulty in transforming experience into a traditional novel. (By contrast, the numerous references to nineteenth-century English writers in *Women in Love* oppose the tradition and solidarity of that period with the chaos and disintegration of the modern age.) But the worst example of Orwell's 'poetic' style is his metamorphosis into a sexual landscape of the countryside where Gordon attempts to seduce Rosemary. While pheasants (which Gordon considers the embodiment of ferocious animal lust) loiter 'with long tails trailing', he says the trees are phallic, the knobs on the bark are 'like the nipples of breasts' and the boughs 'like the wreathing trunks of elephants'. And just before he 'screws himself up' for the effort of seducing the virgin, 'the warm light poured over them as though a membrane across the sky had broken'.

The third major flaw in the novel is the character of the hero, Gordon, who lacks integrity and honour, and whose envy and self-pity tend to alienate the reader's interest. He is selfish and 'horribly unfair' to Rosemary about the use of contraceptives; parasitic with Julia and Ravelston; cowardly with waiters and servants; improvident and lecherous, callous and cold-blooded, without self-respect or principles. But Gordon is more ridiculous and weak than wicked, for Orwell intends him to be an essentially sympathetic hero and suggests that these traits stem less from personality defects than from poverty.

Orwell was well aware of the weaknesses of this novel, but published it anyway because he needed the money. As he wrote in 1946:

> There are two or three books which I am ashamed of and have not allowed to be reprinted or translated, and that [*Keep the Aspidistra Flying*] is one of them. There is an even worse one called *A Clergyman's Daughter*. This was written simply as an exercise and I oughtn't to have published it, but I was desperate for money, ditto when I wrote *Keep the A.* At that time I simply hadn't a book in me, but I was half starved and had to turn out something to bring in £100 or so. (IV.205)

Although Orwell found novel writing a laborious and even agonizing process, he did not consider other (and easier) ways of earning £100.

In spite of these weaknesses in plot, style and characterization, there is undoubtedly a poignant and moving quality about the novel that comes from Orwell's perceptive portrayal of the alienation and loneliness of poverty, and from Rosemary's tender response to Gordon's mean misery. His final affirmation of ordinary life is achieved through her selfless acts: the thrusting of cigarettes in his pocket and her sacrificial sexual surrender. Her love vindicates his self-respect and disproves one of Gordon's *idées fixes*, first stated by Orwell in *Down and Out*: 'There is no doubt that women never, or hardly ever, condescend to men who are much poorer than themselves.'[21]

The novel of poverty is as old as Defoe (Balzac is the French master of this *genre*), but the main English tradition runs from Dickens through Gissing and Orwell (both of whom wrote with insight on Dickens) to John Wain[22] (Orwell's best critic), John Osborne and the 'angry young men', and the plays of Pinter and Wesker. Orwell's acknowledged master and (sometimes baneful) model for the novel of poverty is George Gissing, who wrote that his aim was to depict 'a class of young men distinctive of our time – well educated, fairly bred, but *without money*'.[23] Like Gordon, the writer-hero of Gissing's *New Grub Street* (1891) 'knew what poverty means. The chilling of the brain and heart, the unnerving of the hands, the slow gathering around one of fear and shame and impotent wrath, the dread feeling of helplessness, of the world's base indifference. Poverty! Poverty!'[24] For Orwell, Gissing's 'central theme can be stated in three words – "not enough money". Gissing is the chronicler of poverty ... the cruel, grinding, "respectable" poverty of underfed clerks, downtrodden governesses and bankrupt tradesmen.'[25]

The literary influence of Dostoyevsky is also significant, though perhaps less obvious. The self-tortured and compulsive craving for the lower depths, the self-repudiating and futile 'insulted and injured syndrome', are most powerfully expressed in *Notes From Underground* (1864). Like the underground man, Gordon 'wanted to go down, deep down, into some world where decency no longer mattered; to cut the strings of his self-respect, to submerge himself – to *sink*. ... It was all bound up in his mind with the thought of being *under ground*.'

Orwell's central vision of total grimness and despair, born amidst the sense of approaching disaster in the thirties and intensified by the greater horrors of the forties, is repeated throughout his works like a fatal portent of dissolution and doom. In *Keep the Aspidistra Flying* it is Gordon's vision of the deathliness in modern life, of London slaving under capitalistic oppression, which makes him long for a cleansing holocaust:

> He had a vision of London, of the western world; he saw a thousand million slaves toiling and grovelling about the throne of money. The earth is plowed, ships sail, miners sweat in dripping tunnels underground, clerks hurry for the eight-fifteen with the fear of the boss eating at their vitals. And even in bed with their wives they tremble and obey.[26] Obey whom? The money-priesthood, the pin-faced masters of the world. The Upper Crust.

In *Wigan Pier* it is the vision of the industrial slums of Lancashire, an infinitely depressing grey-black compound of the moon and hell:

> On the outskirts of the mining towns there are frightful landscapes where your horizon is ringed completely round by jagged grey mountains, and underfoot is mud and ashes and overhead the steel cables where the tubs of dirt travel slowly across miles of country. . . . It seemed a world from which vegetation had been banished; nothing existed except smoke, shale, ice, mud, ashes, and foul water.

In *Coming Up For Air*, it is Bowling's vision of an *ersatz* universe completely cut off from any normal and natural sustenance:

> Everything slick and streamlined, everything made out of something else. Celluloid, rubber, chromium-steel everywhere, arc-lamps blazing all night, glass roofs over your head, radios all playing the same tune, no vegetation left, everything cemented over, mock-turtles gazing under neutral fruit-trees.

And in *1984* it is Winston Smith's hopeless vision in the Ministry of Truth – vulgar, squalid, dreary and painfully uncomfortable:

> In any time that he could accurately remember, there had never been quite enough to eat, one had never had socks or underclothes that were not full of holes, furniture had always been battered and rickety, rooms underheated, tube trains crowded, houses falling to pieces, bread dark-coloured, tea a rarity, coffee filthy-tasting, cigarettes insufficient – nothing cheap and plentiful except synthetic gin.

In each of his novels, Orwell contrasts these dreadful visions with joyous scenes of escape from the domination of urban technology to the freedom and simplicity of peaceful nature:[27] Flory meditating in the jungle pool in *Burmese Days*; Dorothy worshipping nature in *A Clergyman's Daughter*; Gordon and Rosemary, Winston and Julia, making love in the countryside in *Keep the Aspidistra Flying* and *1984*; Bowling fishing in *Coming Up For Air*; and the joyous freedom of the animals when they first take over the farm.

This kind of affirmation is also expressed in the conclusion and theme of *Keep the Aspidistra Flying*, after Gordon realizes, like Flory, that one cannot 'live in a corrupt society without being corrupt oneself'. Faced with a choice between the New Albion, the fungus of decaying capitalism, or an abortion for Rosemary, he is secretly relieved to be able to reintegrate himself into a decent, fully human life. But Gordon's movement from a dying to a flying aspidistra is less plausible and too insistently 'symbolic'; and the first stirring of the baby within Rosemary is a sentimental cliché that denies, through its pleasant prognosis, the entire tenor of their unhappy sexual relationship: Gordon's alternation between gross lechery and impotence, Rosemary's frigidity and 'rare sexual desire', and her ultimate 'magnanimous yielding' with neither pleasure nor satisfaction for man or woman. At the end of the novel Gordon decides to link his destiny with the common men who mysteriously transmute the greed and fear of modern civilization into something far nobler. This idealistic commitment represents Orwell's attempt to formulate an acceptable solution to the overwhelming sense of disintegration and decay and to avert the radical pessimism of the late satires, where the possibilities of a decent life are denied.

IV

A number of important ideas from *Keep the Aspidistra Flying* reappear in Orwell's *reportage* of the following year. Gordon's beliefs that poverty kills thought, and that cleanness and decency cost money, are reaffirmed; and the same sense of despair (which culminates in *1984*) is manifest in *Wigan Pier*: 'We live, admittedly, among the wreck of a civilisation.' And Gordon's desire to break out of his family's middle-class insulation and submerge himself in sprawling smoke-dim slums is exactly what Orwell did in *Wigan Pier*.

Though Orwell had never seen these impoverished northern industrial slums before, he knew them well from books. Engels's *The Condition of the Working Classes in England in 1844* (1845), especially the chapter on 'The Mines', Henry Mayhew's *London Labour and the London Poor* (1851) and Charles Booth's *Life and Labour of the People in London* (1889–1903) were his sociological predecessors. Orwell's sympathetic indignation about the injustices suffered by the poor and unemployed is similar to the passionate feelings expressed by the flamboyant Socialist MP Cunninghame Graham. In 1888 Graham defended the rights of the nail- and chain-makers of Cradley Heath, near Birmingham, who worked up to fifteen hours a day for six shillings a week, and wrote:

> I have never gone to Cradley Heath without coming away in the lowest spirits. The mud is the blackest and most clinging, the roads the slushiest and ruttiest, the look of desolation the most appalling, of any place I have ever seen. . . .
> [Cradley Heath represents] failure of civilisation to humanise; failure of commercialism to procure a subsistence; failure of religion to console; failure of Parliament to intervene; failure of individual effort to help; failure of our whole social system.[28]

Dickens's *Hard Times* (1854) and Lawrence's Midlands novels were his literary models. Orwell is obviously drawn to Dickens because of their similar social attitudes, and he repeatedly describes Dickens in a way that forcefully applies to himself as well:

> In every page of his work one can see a consciousness that society is wrong somewhere at the root. (1.416)

> From the whole of Dickens's work one can infer the evil of *laissez-faire* capitalism. (1.417)

[His] 'message' is . . . if men would behave decently the world would be decent. (1.417)

The strongest single impression one carries away from his books is that of a hatred of tyranny. (1.427)

[He is a] man who is always fighting against something, but who fights in the open and is not frightened . . . who is *generously angry*. (1.460)

The very extinction of human vitality and organic life in Orwell's grim vision of Wigan (quoted earlier), is like Dickens's famous description of the mechanical uniformity and unnatural ugliness of Coketown, and Lawrence's portrayal of the insentient corruption of Wiggiston, the mining village that is contrasted to Ursula's hopeful vision of the rainbow.

The economic oppression of the poor also threatens their married and family life. In *Hard Times*, the 'hateful' Bounderby tells the worker Stephen Blackpool, 'You had better have been satisfied as you were, and not got married';[29] and the ironic conversation of Bitzer and Mrs Sparsit expresses the selfish and moribund attitude of the middle classes:

'I am quite sure we are constantly hearing, ma'am, till it becomes quite nauseous, concerning their wives and families,' said Bitzer. 'Why look at me, ma'am! *I* don't want a wife and family. Why should they?'
'Because they are improvident,' said Mrs Sparsit.[30]

It is precisely this view, so hostile to human needs, that Orwell attacks in both *Keep the Aspidistra Flying* and *Wigan Pier*. In the former, Gordon (who violently, and unfairly, objects to Rosemary's wish for contraceptives) says, 'Hats off to the factory lad who with fourpence in the world puts his girl in a family way! At least he's got blood and not money in his veins'; and Orwell writes in the latter, alluding to Walter Greenwood's popular play of 1933, 'Getting married on the dole annoys old ladies in Brighton, but it is a proof of their essential good sense; they realize that losing your job does not mean that you cease to be a human being.' In *The Rainbow* (1915), the colliery manager Tom Brangwen, who exploits the miners, marries the lesbian school mistress Winifred Inger, a strange union of perversion, sterility and corruption. And in *Women in Love* (1920) and *Lady Chatterley's Lover* (1928), the ugliness, poverty and suffering that Gerald Crich and Clifford Chatterley inflict on the miners is symptomatic of their radical failure as human beings. In Dickens, Lawrence and Orwell, the emotional sterility of the mine owners is contrasted to the inextinguishable warmth and vitality of the oppressed working people, and reflected in the deathly ugliness of the landscape: 'The car ploughed uphill through the long squalid straggle of Tevershall, the blackened brick dwellings, the black slate roofs glistening their sharp edges, the mud black with coal-dust, the pavements wet and black. It was as if dismalness had soaked through and through everything.'[31]

In the 1930s coal 'was by far the largest single industry, the only one employing more than a million workers. It had always been the symbol of class struggle.'[32] Orwell's immersion in the reality of this struggle was his very deliberate attempt to overcome what he considered 'the tragic failure of theoretical Socialism, to make contact with the normal working classes'.[33] Orwell believes it is both his duty and his responsibility to have first-hand experience in the slums and mines, and he cannot see the value of the more objective intellectual inquiry of Beatrice Webb, whom he calls a 'high-minded Socialist slum visitor'. As he wrote to Richard Rees from Wigan, 'Have you ever been down a mine? I don't think I shall ever feel quite the same about coal again' (1.164). Orwell's acute observations on coal mining leave a vivid impression, for his farmer's knowledge of the earth and his Swiftian ability to isolate the significant detail of the grazing cows make you see mining in a new and memorable way: 'You have a tolerable sized mountain on top of you; hundreds of yards of solid rock, bones of extinct beasts, subsoil, flints, roots of growing things, green grass and cows grazing on it – all this suspended over your head and held back only by wooden props as thick as the calf of your leg.' And his account of the miners crawling to work underground for two or three hours each day – without pay – is a powerful and disturbing revelation.

Orwell's approach is documentary, empirical and pragmatic, filled with statistics, essential information and useful suggestions, and his view is, as far as possible, an 'insider's' view.[34] In praising people's patience with him, Orwell humorously describes his methods and their response:

> If any unauthorised person walked into *my* house and began asking me whether the roof leaked and whether I was much troubled by bugs and what I thought of my landlord, I should probably tell him to go to hell. This only happened to me once, and in that case the woman was slightly deaf and took me for a Means Test nark; but even she relented after a while and gave me the information I wanted.

Orwell constantly refers to his own practical knowledge ('you can wring forty cups of tea out of a quarter-pound packet') with phrases like 'I have had just enough experience . . .', 'From my own observation . . .' and 'Once when I was . . .'. The result of this approach is twofold: as in *Down and Out* he questions common assumptions, discredits the illusion and shows the reality; and he also describes the most serious injustices as he has lived through them himself. He has a deep loathing of the ugliness, emptiness and cruelty of what he sees, but is not merely content to describe it – he wants to make people feel morally responsible so that they will radically change it.[35]

The main effect of shattering illusions and enforcing reality is to convince the reader that he is profoundly ill-informed and must change his wrong-headed attitude about the working classes. Contrary to popular belief, Orwell finds that miners wash when they can; eat astonishingly little; are poorly paid; have impoverished landlords who cannot afford repairs; *do* mind dirtiness; favour slum clearance; dislike crowded areas; want to work and do not like unemployment; are sensitive and serious; do not smell; and lead an extremely hard life. In short, they are much like other people ('the interests of the exploited are the same'), only worse off because of the inequity and iniquity of the capitalist system. By making readers understand the workers, Orwell alleviates their fears and engages their sympathy; by making them *care* about their countrymen, he pricks their social conscience and awakens their sense of justice.

The great strength of *Wigan Pier* (and *Down and Out*) is that the economic injustices are always described in human terms. Orwell's vision of Wigan is like Blake's of London:

> Mark in every face I meet
> Marks of weakness, marks of woe,

and for both writers a slum implies warped lives and ailing children. Orwell's moving theme is a fervent plea for human dignity and compassion, and against 'The frightful doom of a decent working man suddenly thrown on the streets after a lifetime of steady work, his agonized struggles against economic laws which he does not understand, the disintegration of families, the corroding sense of shame.' He attacks Corporation housing because it is soulless and inhumane, and erodes both family and communal life; he criticizes the Means Test because it cruelly breaks up families; and he exposes the deadening effect of unemployment. His images of human degradation are the most powerful: the desolate drudgery of the exhausted young woman kneeling beside the blocked waste-pipe; the blank and aged grandmother with the yellow cretinous countenance; the worn skull-like face of the slum mother; and the dumpy shawled women crawling in the cindery mud in search of coal chips. (Orwell's contrasting image of human affirmation is the pavement-artist Bozo in *Down and Out*, who gazes at the stars and is a free man in his own mind: 'rich or poor, you can still keep on with your books and your ideas'.[36]) Orwell's emphasis throughout the book is on the 'ordinary decent person', and the sense of human waste, shame and debasement that he conveys is overwhelming. As Orwell wrote during the War, 'I hate to see England either humiliated or humiliating anybody else.... I wanted to think that the class distinctions and imperialist exploitation of which I am ashamed would not return' (III.297).

Though Orwell writes, 'I have seen just enough of the working class to avoid idealizing them', and dissociates himself from a belief in the superiority of the proletariat, he also idealizes the manners, temperament, stoicism, family life and democracy of the working class.[37] This is partly because he is intensely dissatisfied with his own middle-class origins and wants to transcend them. But more importantly, he feels, like Malraux, Sartre and other French writers of the thirties, that the working class 'incarnates some deeply meaningful myth of suffering, and that in its emancipation lies the general "salvation of mankind"'.[38] Victor Brombert's analysis of the basic attitudes of French intellectuals toward Marxist beliefs applies with equal force to Orwell's ethic of responsibility:

> 1. a characteristic, nearly pathological *humility* in the face of the Proletariat. . . . 2. the belief that the bourgeois intellectual can save his soul only by sharing the suffering of the working class and by imitating its 'Passion'. . . . 3. the conviction that any present sacrifices, even self-destruction, will be eschatologically justified; that the intellectual's duty is to prepare the future. . . . 4. the concomitant quest for holiness by means of martyrdom.[39]

(The fourth point is implicit in the imitation of the 'Passion' and the sacrificial self-destruction.)

Orwell is quite explicit about his humility: 'If there is one type of man to whom I feel myself inferior, it is a coal miner'; and partly because he was weak and unhealthy, he exhibits an almost Lawrencean admiration for their earthiness and physical power: 'underground, blackened to the eyes, with their throats full of coal dust, driving their shovels forward with arms and belly muscles of steel'. Orwell is equally clear on the idea of penitential sacrifice among the 'symbolic victims': 'I wanted to submerge myself, to get right down among the oppressed, to be one of them on their side against the tyrants. . . . Once I had been among them and accepted by them, I should have touched bottom . . . and part of my guilt would drop from me.'

The third point is twofold: the duty to prepare the future and the idea of self-punishment. The whole force of Orwell's argument for 'the ideal of Socialism, justice and liberty' testifies to his desire to prepare for the future, 'to push the world in a certain direction, to alter other people's idea of the kind of society that they should strive after' (1.4). And his entire career, a compulsive pattern of idealistic sacrifices in Burma, France, Spain and England, reveals his quest for self-punishment.

Orwell's belief in personal sacrifice was recorded in his diary during the grim days of June 1940 when England was threatened by a German invasion, and these words express, perhaps more than anything else he wrote, his personal courage and high moral principle:

> Both E and G insistent that I should go to Canada if the worst comes to the worst, in order to stay alive and keep up the propaganda. I will go if I have some function, e.g. if the government were transferred to Canada and I had some kind of job, but not as a refugee, not as an expatriate journalist squealing from a safe distance. There are too many of these exiled 'anti-Fascists' already. Better to die if necessary, and maybe even as propaganda one's death might achieve more than going abroad and living more or less unwanted on other people's charity. (II.355)[40]

But there is a note of desperation in this passage, for the outbreak of the War at the end of the decade marks Orwell's retreat from his positive and melioristic works of the thirties, which culminated in his conversion to Socialism in 1936, to his more negative and pessimistic satires of the forties. He laments in 1940, for example, about 'The unspeakable depression of lighting the fires every morning with papers of a year ago, and getting glimpses of optimistic headlines as they go up in smoke' (II.377). Orwell shares the Marxist concept of the dissolution of capitalistic society – the apocalyptic war predicted in *Coming Up For Air* broke out three months after the book was published – but not its optimistic belief in the creation of a new and better one.

Orwell says some rather harsh things about his Socialist colleagues in what he liked to call 'pansy-left circles', and when *The Road to Wigan Pier* was published in 1937 (while Orwell was in Spain) the publisher, Victor Gollancz, added a Foreword that attempted to draw the venom from Orwell's sting and to pacify the outraged sentiments of the members of the Left Book Club.

Orwell's statement that 'One sometimes gets the impression that the mere words "Socialism" and "Communism" draw towards them with magnetic force every fruit-juice drinker, nudist, sandal-wearer, sex-maniac, Quaker, "Nature Cure" quack, pacifist, and feminist in England' seems deliberately provocative. But he is actually attacking the disciples of that crank and crusader, Edward Carpenter, who embodied most of these characteristics. For Carpenter (1844–1929), who had a significant influence on both E. M. Forster and D. H. Lawrence, was a social reformer, pioneer of return to rural simplicity, militant homosexual (in the tradition of Walt Whitman), and author of books like *Civilisation: Its Cause and Cure* (1889) and *The Intermediate Sex* (1908). Gollancz, anxious to dissociate Socialism from sodomy, warns that the deluded Orwell 'is still a victim of that early atmosphere in his home and public school', that he gives 'a distorted picture of what Socialists are like and what they say' and 'seems to suggest that almost every Socialist is a "crank" '.[41]

Orwell also attacks the 'machine-worship and the stupid cult of Russia', and states: 'The unfortunate thing is that Socialism, as usually presented, is bound up with the idea of mechanical progress, not merely as a necessary development but as an end in itself, almost as a kind of religioh.' And Gollancz, who anticipates Marxist critics of *Animal Farm* and *1984*, blindly refuses to recognize the brutal methods used by Stalin to achieve industrialization and states: 'Amongst the grave faults which Mr Orwell finds in Socialist propaganda is the glorification of industrialism and in particular the triumphs of industrialization in the Soviet Union. . . . [But his criticism] hardly carries conviction, when the achievements of the Soviet Union are there for everyone to see.' Gollancz also condemns Orwell for committing 'the curious indiscretion of referring to Russian commissars as "half-gramophones, half-gangsters" '.[42]

Beginning with *Coming Up For Air*, the intensity of Orwell's severity and grief recalls the lamentations of an Old Testament prophet. 'If one looks back over the past quarter of a century,' Orwell writes in 1945, 'one finds that there was hardly a single year when atrocity stories were not being reported from some part of the world' (III.370).[43] 'Wherever one looks one sees fiercer struggles than the Crusades, worse tyrannies than the Inquisition and bigger lies than the Popish Plot.'[44] Unlike the people living before 1914, who had the advantage of not knowing the War was coming or at least not foreseeing what it would be like, Orwell has 'known since about 1931 . . . that the future must be catastrophic. . . . Since about 1934 I have known that war between England and Germany was coming, and since 1936 I have known it with complete certainty' (II.345–6). *Coming Up For Air* is Orwell's *Götterdämmerung*, the expression of his greatest fears.

5   Orwell's Apocalypse:
Coming Up For Air

> They were born after 1914 and are therefore
> incapable of happiness.
>
> BERTRAND RUSSELL

Coming Up For Air (1939), Orwell's central transitional work, is at
once synthetic and seminal, gathering the themes that had been
explored in the poverty books of the thirties and anticipating the
cultural essays and political satires of the next decade. The location
and central symbol of the novel appear as early as *Down and Out*
when Orwell describes tramping in Lower Binfield and fishing in
the Seine; but the novel has much closer affinities with *Keep the
Aspidistra Flying*, for Gordon Comstock's belief that our civilization
is dying and the whole world will soon be blown up is very like
Bowling's. Similarly, Comstock's fulmination against marriage
and his dreadful vision of a million fearful slaves grovelling before
the throne of money are repeated in the later novel. Comstock's
fellow-lodger and sometime friend, the travelling salesman Flaxman, has the same good humour, stout physique and mild vanity of
Bowling; and he too uses some extra money to escape from his wife.

The dull, shabby, dead-alive Comstock family, who depressingly
dwell in an atmosphere of semi-genteel failure, resemble the decayed
middle-class family of Hilda Bowling whose vitality has been
sapped by poverty. Like the Oxford don Porteous, whose name
suggests old wine and Latin, they live 'inside the whale', entirely
in the dead world of the past. When everything else has changed for

the worse, only Hilda's fossilized Anglo-Indian family and the eternally classical Porteous have stayed the same, and their political vacuum has been filled by the hateful Left Book Club lecturer: 'All the decent people are paralysed. Dead men and live gorillas.'[1] As Yeats writes in 'The Second Coming', 'The best lack all conviction, while the worst/ Are full of passionate intensity.'

The Road to Wigan Pier satirizes many of the same subjects as this novel: drab and soulless estate housing, mild and mindless Socialists, the crankish fruit-juice drinker, nudist and sandal-wearer of Pixy Glen, and the difficulty of finding unpolluted streams with live fish in them. And one of the most striking images of working-class life in *Wigan Pier* is repeated in *Coming Up*. The decrepit woman who had 'the usual exhausted face of the slum girl who is twenty-five and looks forty, thanks to miscarriages and drudgery'[2] becomes Bowling's boyhood nursemaid: 'A wrinkled-up hag of a woman, with her hair coming down and a smoky face, looking at least fifty years old. . . . It was Katie, who must have been twenty-seven.' As in *Wigan Pier*, the deterioration and decay of the natural landscape is paralleled by a similar decline that Bowling observes in people. In the early twenties, Hilda Bowling was a 'pretty, delicate girl . . . and within only about three years she's settled down into a depressed, lifeless, middle-aged frump'. When he returns to Binfield in the thirties, Elsie, his first love, 'with her milky-white skin and red mouth and kind of dull-gold hair, had turned into this great round-shouldered hag, shambling along on twisted heels'.

Finally, Orwell's idealization of domestic life in *Wigan Pier* is repeated in the novel when Bowling's parents read the Sunday newspaper:

> A Sunday afternoon – summer, of course, always summer – a smell of roast pork and greens still floating in the air, and Mother on one side of the fireplace, starting off to read the latest murder but gradually falling asleep with her mouth open, and Father on the other, in slippers and spectacles, working his way slowly through yards of smudgy print . . . and myself under the table with the B.O.P. [Boys' Own Paper], making believe that the tablecloth is a tent.

This Dickensian description of sentimental and soporific, cosy and mindless domestic dullness would be used satirically by most modern writers, but Orwell portrays the scene from the point of view of a secure and protected child.

Bowling's prophetic fears about the destruction of his childhood England by bombs follow inevitably from Orwell's ambivalent thoughts in the final paragraph of *Homage to Catalonia* as he returns to England:

> Down here it was still the England I had known in my childhood: the railway-cuttings smothered in wild flowers, the deep meadows where the great shining horses browse and meditate, the slow-moving streams bordered by willows, the green bosoms of the elms, the larkspurs in the cottage gardens . . . all sleeping the deep sleep of England, from which I sometimes fear that we shall never wake till we are jerked out of it by the roar of bombs.

Orwell says that 'the phrase that Hitler coined for the Germans, "a sleep-walking people", would have been better applied to the English' (II.58), and the somnolence of this pleasant pastoral nostalgia is clearly related to the drowsy numbness of mother and father at the fireplace.

Coming Up For Air is about an apocalyptic vision that destroys a nostalgic dream of childhood. For Bowling is in a prophetic mood in which he foresees the end of the world and can feel things cracking and collapsing under his feet. The war that will decide the destiny of Europe is due in 1941, and it seems to Bowling (as it did to Orwell at the end of *Homage*) that he 'could see the whole of England, and all the people in it, and all the things that will happen to all of them'. Bowling, caught in a brief intense moment between the destructive future and the nostalgic past, seeks, like Winston Smith, to escape the painful modern realities by recapturing his idealized childhood memories. Orwell's metaphor of escape in both works (people trapped in a sinking ship is the symbol of man's fate in *1984*) is 'coming up for air', 'like the big sea-turtles when they come paddling up to the surface, stick their noses out and fill their lungs with a treat gulp before they sink down again among the seaweed and octopuses'. But escape is impossible for Bowling, who has the archetypal experience of returning home to discover that the lost Eden of childhood is irrecoverable: 'What's the good of trying to revisit the scenes of your boyhood? They don't exist. Coming up for air! But there isn't any air. The dustbin we're in reaches up to the stratosphere.'

The childhood passages of *Coming Up* have the same affectionate and nostalgic tone as Orwell's 'As I Please' column and his major essays on English popular culture, like 'Boys' Weeklies'. These essays, which develop and illuminate the themes of the novel, were written against the background of the Second World War. In one of these cultural essays, 'The Art of Donald McGill' (1941), Orwell lists the conventions of the comic postcard jokes – all women plot marriage, which only benefits women; all husbands are henpecked; middle-aged men are drunkards; nudism is comical; Air Raid precautions are ludicrous; illegitimate babies and old maids are always funny (II.157–9) – and nearly every one of them appears in *Coming Up*. Actually, Bowling's colloquial humour is far superior to these conventional jokes. He 'baptises' his new false teeth in a pub, compares Hilda's constriction to that of an 'average zenana', says that one old lady thought the Left Book Club had to do with books left in railway carriages, and observes that he got fat 'so suddenly that it was as if a cannon ball had hit me and got stuck inside'. Orwell's description of Bowling guarding the tins of bully-beef in Cornwall (an allusion to his father's military service in the Great War), and especially his satire on Hilda's (and his own) Anglo-Indian family and on Porteous, both mummified relics of the past, is well done. *Coming Up*, like *Gem* and *Magnet*, *Raffles* (all three are mentioned in the novel), comic postcards, *Helen's Babies*, Bertie Wooster and Jeeves, and 'Good Bad Books', recreates a decent, stable, familiar, but non-existent world.

In each of his essays on popular culture, Orwell favourably compares the static old-fashioned view expressed in these works with that of their harsher and crueller successors: the schoolboy atmosphere of *Raffles* and 'Boys' Weeklies' with the torture and corruption of *No Orchids for Miss Blandish* and the 'Yank mags', the classic perfect poison murder with the modern bloody 'Cleft Chin Murder'. (The closing paragraphs of 'Raffles' and 'Decline' are nearly identical.) All these popular works are Orwell's boyhood favourites, have a strictly pre-war outlook, and never mention contemporary politics. Popular books like *Helen's Babies* and *Little Women* 'have something that is perhaps best described as integrity, or good morale' (IV.246). Their world, like that of Lower Binfield at the turn of the century, was more class-ridden and more impoverished than the modern world, but did not have an oppressive sense of helplessness. As Orwell says in an unpublished BBC talk,

> What you are not likely to find in the mind of anyone in the year 1900, is a doubt about the continuity of civilisation. If the world as people saw it then was rather harsh, simple and slow-moving, it was also secure. Things would continue in a more or less recognisable pattern; life might not get appreciably more pleasant, but at any rate barbarism wouldn't return.[3]

This opposition between past and present is symbolized by the house in Binfield that is cleaved by the accidental bomb: 'What was extraordinary was that in the upstairs rooms nothing had been touched ... but the lower rooms had caught the force of the explosion. There was a frightful smashed-up mess.' Both the pre-war past and the warlike present have rather obvious contrasting characteristics. In old Lower Binfield there was no rush and no fear, in West Bletchley everyone is 'scared stiff'; in the past the aeroplane was 'a flimsy, rickety-looking thing', in the present threatening bombers constantly fly overhead; in the pre-war world fish swim in the pond, in the modern world, writes John Wain, 'fish is the stuff they put into sausages instead of meat':[4]

> Ersatz, they call it. I remembered reading that *they* were making sausages out of fish, and fish, no doubt, out of something different. It gave me the feeling that I'd bitten into the modern world and discovered what it was really made of. ... But when you come down to brass tacks and get your [false] teeth into something solid, a sausage for instance, that's what you get. Rotten fish in a rubber skin. Bombs of filth bursting inside your mouth.

The explosive and perverse phallic image emphasizes the corruption and sterility of Lower Binfield. Orwell frequently protests against 'the instinctive horror which all sensitive people feel at the progressive mechanisation of life' (IV.81); and in one of his rare poems, 'On a Ruined Farm near the His Master's Voice Gramophone Factory', he grieves that 'The acid smoke has soured the fields,/ And browned the few and windworn flowers' (I.135). These lines echo the tradition that goes back to Blake, and that has been voiced most powerfully in the modern age by Lawrence (in *Lady Chatterley's Lover*) and by Forster, whose views in *Abinger Pageant* (1934) are similar to Orwell's:

> Houses and bungalows, hotels, restaurants and flats, arterial roads, by-passes, petrol pumps and pylons – are these going to be England? Are these man's final triumph? Or is there another England, green and eternal, which will outlast them?[5]

Orwell's symbol of England's green and pleasant land is fishing, 'the opposite of war', and so much of the novel is concerned with fishing that Orwell might have subtitled his book, which takes place near Walton, *The Compleat Angler*. Yet it remains an effective symbol:

> The very idea of sitting all day under a willow tree beside a quiet pool – and being able to find a quiet pool to sit beside – belongs to the time before the war. . . . There's a kind of peacefulness even in the names of English coarse fish. . . . They're solid kinds of names.

The ideal fishing pool is the secret one behind Binfield House where enormous carp, perhaps a hundred years old, sun themselves near the tranquil surface of the water. When Bowling finally returns there, he finds the Thames crowded and polluted and the sacred pool a drained cavern half full of tin cans.

Isaac Rosenfeld's shrewd observation that Orwell was 'a radical in politics and a conservative in feeling',[6] both a socialist and a man in love with the past, explains why Orwell is so deeply ambivalent about the pre-war period. He criticizes the English for 'obstinately clinging to everything that is out of date and a nuisance '(II.58), but creates an ideal pub, 'The Moon under Water', in which 'everything has the solid comfortable ugliness of the nineteenth century' (III.45). He praises the postcards of Donald McGill, for 'there is no sign in them of any attempt to induce an outlook acceptable to the ruling class' (II.159), but he calls 'Boys' Weeklies' 'sodden in the worst illusions of 1910' because they inculcate pernicious social and political attitudes: the boys 'get what they are looking for, but they get it wrapped up in the illusions which their future employers think suitable for them' (I.484, 482). In 'England Your England' he states that both the common people and the intellectuals must and do oppose the existing social order, yet he also attacks the pre-war world of 'Boys' Weeklies' that is very similar in mood to his description of Lower Binfield:

> The year is 1910. . . . There is a cosy fire in the study, and outside the wind is whistling. The ivy clusters thickly round the old grey stones. The King is on his throne and the pound is worth a pound. . . . Everything is safe, solid and unquestionable. Everything will be the same for ever and ever. (I.473)

Since Orwell believes 'one of the dominant facts in English life during the past three-quarters of a century has been the decay of ability in the ruling class' (II.69), and since all the peace and serenity of pre-war England depends on the leisure of the few and the labour of the many, he admires the working, lower-middle and middle-class aspects of the pre-war world but attacks the upper-middle and upper-class characteristics. In 'Such, Such Were the Joys', Orwell ambivalently criticizes and cherishes the decent but rather decadent 'age of *The Merry Widow*, Saki's novels and *Peter Pan*' and describes the

> atmosphere, as it were, of eating everlasting strawberry ices on green lawns to the tune of the Eton Boating Song. The extraordinary thing was the way in which everyone took it for granted that this oozing, bulging wealth of the English upper and upper-middle classes would last forever, and was part of the order of things. After 1918 it was never quite the same again. (IV.357)

And in *Coming Up*, *Pixy* Glen, like *Wendy's* Tea Shoppe, represents a spurious attempt by the lower-middle classes to climb upwards by returning to the artificiality of Barrie's pre-war world.

'I am not able, and I do not want, completely to abandon the world-view that I acquired in childhood' writes Orwell (I.6); and when, in the summer of 1940, he escaped into the country with his dog Marx and had two glorious days at Wallington, 'the whole thing took me straight back to my childhood, perhaps the last bit of that kind of life that I shall ever have' (II.366). Though Orwell yearns to return to his boyhood years, it is rather difficult to reconcile his childhood nostalgia with the grim tortures of 'Such, Such Were the Joys'. It would seem that this ideal childhood existed only in Orwell's imagination, and that his works represent a fairly consistent attempt to recreate and perpetuate this myth.

Orwell has a keen desire to establish a continuity between the England of the past and that of the present, and is particularly attracted to writers who, like T. S. Eliot, carry on the human heritage by 'keeping in touch with pre-war emotions' (I.524–5). The most perfect embodiment of the pre-war myth of eternal ease and blue summer skies is Brooke's 'The Old Vicarage, Grantchester' (1912), and in 'The Captain's Doll' (1923) Lawrence also writes with retrospective nostalgia about these peaceful years which 'seemed lovely, almost like before the war: almost the same feeling of eternal holiday, as if the world was made for man's everlasting holiday'.[7] Reviewing Edmund Blunden's *Cricket Country*, Orwell states that 'the essential thing in this book, as in nearly everything that Mr Blunden writes, is his nostalgia for the golden age before 1914, when the world was peaceful as it has never since been' (III.48); and he says almost the same thing about H. G. Wells, whose greatest gift 'was his power to convey the atmosphere of the golden years between 1890 and 1914'.[8] Wells's *The History of Mr. Polly* (1910) has a strong effect on Bowling and, as Orwell says of *Coming Up* in a letter to Julian Symons, 'Of course the book was bound to suggest Wells watered down. I have a great admiration for Wells, i.e. as a writer, and he was a very early influence on me' (IV.422).

This golden tranquillity was shattered forever by the kind of modern war that Bowling experienced in Flanders and Orwell fought in Spain. The unrefrigerated backyard of the Binfield butcher 'smelt like a battlefield'; the ravaged landscape of 'tin cans, turds, mud, weeds, clumps of rusty barbed wire' is exactly like the catalogue of the Aragon front; both Orwell and Bowling try to escape war by fishing; and the description of Bowling's explosive wound derives from that day at Huesca when Orwell was shot through the throat. Bowling believes that, if war did not kill you, it was bound to make you think about the kind of world that would emerge from the ruins, and some aspects of the world of *1984* already exist in *Coming Up*: the blunt razor-blades, the nasty gusts of wind, the vision of the seedy, smashed streets. Bowling finds a severed leg at a bomb site just as Winston Smith finds a severed hand; and, like Winston, the cringing victims in the housing estate lick the hand that wallops them. The red-armed and fertile-bellied prole washerwoman is foreshadowed by Bowling's peaceful glimpse of the roofs where the women hang out the washing, and the 'Two Minutes of Hate' is anticipated by the enraged *anti*-Fascist (a nice touch) lecturer at the Left Book Club. Bowling fears the post-war totalitarian State even more than the cataclysmic war, and the Oceania of *1984* is foreshadowed in *Coming Up*:

> *It's all going to happen.* All the things you've got at the back of your mind, the things you're terrified of, the things you tell yourself are just a night-mare or only happen in foreign countries. The bombs, the food-queues, the rubber truncheons, the barbed wire, the coloured shirts, the slogans, the enormous faces, the machine-guns squirting out of bedroom windows.

Orwell's apocalyptic belief is similar to Henry Miller's, who told Orwell that 'Our civilisation was destined to be swept away and replaced by something so different that we should scarcely regard it as human. . . . Everywhere there is the sense of the approaching cataclysm' (I.519). Miller made a powerful impression on Orwell, and his astonishing indifference and passivity about the impending doom was both fascinating and deeply attractive. Miller, perhaps more than any other modern writer, totally rejects Orwell's concept of decency, his vague but important term for the synthesis of the traditional English virtues that he describes in 'England Your England': gentleness, fairness, integrity, unselfishness, comradeship, patriotism, respect for legality, belief in justice, liberty and truth. In the world of modern power politics, especially as Orwell describes it, these qualities barely survive: they exist in Wiltshire perhaps, but not in Whitehall. One of his major weaknesses is that he puts too much faith in this ineffectual and disappearing decency, for decent men seldom achieve political power, and if they do, they rarely remain decent. Yet Orwell feels the need to believe in *something* – 'The real problem is how to restore the religious attitude while accepting death as final' (III.244) – and there is nothing else left to believe in *but* decency.

Miller's extreme immorality and sensuality and his imaginative intensity are precisely the qualities that Orwell lacks, and his social radicalism is characteristically American just as Orwell's conservatism is typically English. Orwell's profound and ambiguous attraction (revealed in his long essay and three enthusiastic book reviews on Miller) to someone who could remain so oblivious and insulated illuminates his strange ambivalence about preserving the past and about his intense commitment to the concept of decency.

Like Miller, James Joyce also rejects decency and remains supremely indifferent to modern politics. As Orwell says, Joyce wrote *Ulysses* 'in Switzerland, with an Austrian passport and a British pension, during the 1914–18 war, to which he paid as nearly as possible no attention' (III.107). Orwell is extremely enthusiastic about *Ulysses*, studies it carefully and writes about it frequently. In a letter of 1933 he states, 'Joyce interests me so much that I can't stop talking about him once I start' (I.128); and the following year he makes a witty comparison between himself and the author of *Ulysses* (1922) in a Joycean sexual-musical image:

> When I read a book like that and then come back to my own work, I feel like a eunuch who has taken a course in voice production and can

pass himself off fairly well as a bass or baritone, but if you listen closely
you can hear the good old squeak just the same as ever. (1.139)

Orwell's novel has several Joycean echoes. The firm of Wilson &
Bloom builds houses on Bowling's street; Orwell's epigraph, 'He's
dead, but he won't lie down' recalls the song 'Finnegan's Wake';
and Bowling reads Molly's favourite author, Paul de Kock.

Orwell's many statements about *Ulysses* illuminate the central
theme of his own novel – the lost world of childhood and the despair
of ordinary people in the modern world – as well as the personality
and character of Bowling, who is modelled on Leopold Bloom:

> Here is a whole world of stuff which you have lived with since child-
> hood, stuff which you supposed to be of its nature incommunicable, and
> somebody has managed to communicate it. The effect is to break down,
> at any rate momentarily, the solitude in which the human being lives.
> When you read certain passages in *Ulysses* you feel that Joyce's mind and
> your mind are one, that he knows all about you though he has never
> heard your name, that there·exists some world outside time and space
> in which you and he are together. And though he does not resemble
> Joyce in other ways, there is a touch of this quality in Henry Miller.
> (1.495)

> [*Ulysses*] sums up better than any book I know the fearful despair that
> is almost normal in modern times. (1.121)

> Books about ordinary people behaving in an ordinary manner are
> extremely rare, because they can only be written by someone who is
> capable of standing both inside and outside the ordinary man, as Joyce
> for instance stands inside and outside Bloom. (1.230)

> [Bloom has] a streak of intellectual curiosity. . . . [He] is a rather excep-
> tionally sensitive specimen of the man in the street, and I think the
> especial interest of this is that the cultivated man and the man in the street
> so rarely meet in modern literature. (1.127–8)

Orwell describes Bowling as being, like Bloom, 'rather thoughtful
and fairly well-educated, even slightly bookish' (1.358). Though
Bloom and Bowling (their names are similar though Bowling
suggests the bourgeois bowler hat) are not comparable in depth of
characterization (the bass and the eunuch), and Bowling is more

brash and hardened, they both are intelligent, curious, perceptive, sympathetic, good-natured, humorous and vulgar, and both are nostalgic about a happier past. Both characters are 'ordinary middling chaps' and both are salesmen, though Bowling is more successful and feels superior to the two newspaper canvassers (Bloom's job) whom he meets on the train to London. Both know many obscure 'scientific' facts; Bowling's mind, like Bloom's, 'goes in jerks'; and the thought of the Albanian King Zog 'starts memories' of King Og of Bashan and transports Bowling back to his 'incommunicable' childhood through a Joycean 'stream of consciousness' that attempts to capture the past:

> The past is a curious thing. It's with you all the time. I suppose an hour never passes without your thinking of things that happened ten or twenty years ago. . . . Then some chance sight or sound or smell, especially smell, sets you going, and the past doesn't merely come back to you, you're actually *in* the past.

In 1948 Orwell responded to Julian Symons's criticism of *Coming Up*, and said: 'Of course you are perfectly right about my own character constantly intruding on that of the narrator. I am not a real novelist anyway, and that particular vice is inherent in writing a novel in the first person, which one should never do' (IV.422). This frank admission of his lack of imaginative power (and his need to write for money) explains why Orwell's books have so much in common and why his novels are so often nourished by his essays. It also explains his eager receptivity to the influence of Joyce and of D. H. Lawrence, whom he also alludes to in his novel.

A man named Mellors gives Bowling the racing tip that provides his escape money; and, like Lawrence's Mellors, Bowling rises to the officer class during the war and becomes, temporarily, a gentleman. Lawrence's story 'The Thorn in the Flesh' is referred to in the novel, and Bowling enjoys reading *Sons and Lovers*. More significantly, the mood of *Coming Up*, and indeed of many of Orwell's works of the thirties, is close to the opening sentences of *Lady Chatterley's Lover* – 'Ours is essentially a tragic age, so we refuse to take it

tragically. The cataclysm has happened, we are among the ruins'
and to the dark prophecies of Lawrence's letters:

> I am so sad, for my country, for this great wave of civilisation, 2000
> years, which is now collapsing, that it is hard to live. So much beauty and
> pathos of old things passing away and no new things coming ... the
> winter stretches ahead, where all vision is lost and all memory dies out.[9]

A disintegrating civilization on the verge of an annihilating war
has been the subject of the greatest novels of our time – *Women in
Love*, *Remembrance of Things Past*, *The Magic Mountain* – and
Coming Up For Air belongs *thematically* with these books. Written
a generation later, the novel conveys many of the modes of thought
and feeling characteristic of Orwell's age – the uncertainty, fear and
despair that are expressed in Spengler's *Decline of the West* and Yeats's
'The Second Coming', in Miller's *Tropic of Cancer* and Auden's
'September 1, 1939'. As Leonard Woolf writes in his autobiography:

> In 1914 in the background of one's life and one's mind there were light
> and hope; by 1918 one had unconsciously accepted a perpetual public
> menace and darkness and had admitted in the privacy of one's mind or
> soul an iron fatalistic acquiescence in insecurity and barbarism.[10]

While working on *Coming Up* Orwell writes to Cyril Connolly
in Gadarene imagery: 'Everything one writes now is overshadowed
by this ghastly feeling that we are rushing towards a precipice and,
though we shan't actually prevent ourselves or anyone else from
going over, must put up some sort of fight' (1.362). Despite the grim
prognostications, Bowling opposes the threatening cataclysm. His
imaginative preservation of the past is the positive core in the novel
that survives the present horrors and ultimately conveys the most
powerful effect in the book. As Bowling says, 'I'm fat but I'm thin
inside. Has it ever struck you that there's a thin man [the past]
inside every fat man [the present]?' This preservation of the past
in the free minds of helpless yet resisting men will be one of Orwell's
central concerns in both *Animal Farm* and *1984*. These books grew
directly out of his intensely disillusioning experiences in the Spanish
Civil War, which he recorded in *Homage to Catalonia*.

6 'An Affirming Flame':
Homage to Catalonia

> May I, composed like them
> Of Eros and of dust
> Beleaguered by the same
> Negation and despair
> Show an affirming flame.
>   W. H. AUDEN, 'September 1, 1939'

PASSING THROUGH PARIS on his way to fight in Spain in 1936, Orwell stopped to meet Henry Miller, whose books he had reviewed and admired. Miller cared nothing for the Spanish War, and forcefully told Orwell, who was going to combat Fascism and defend democracy *from a sense of obligation* (1.519), that he was an idiot. This striking confrontation reveals the polarity of political attitudes among modern writers. If Miller, as Orwell later wrote, is undoubtedly 'inside the whale' – performing 'the essential Jonah act of allowing himself to be swallowed, remaining passive, *accepting*' (1.521)[1] – then Orwell himself is clearly 'outside the whale', responsible, active, rejecting the horrors of the modern world and committing himself to change them. He is part of the collective tragedy and shares in the collective guilt, and he would agree with Dostoyevsky that 'every one is really responsible to all men for all men and for everything'.[2] This belief made Orwell feel guilt and responsibility on behalf of others who did *not* feel it. Spain was the magnet that attracted such writers as Orwell, Malraux and Hemingway, intellectual men of letters who were also men of war, the very incarnation of the heroes they created in their books.

In his valuable essay, 'Orwell in Perspective', John Wain states that much of the criticism on Orwell is useless or misdirected because it 'started out from the wrong end. It is impossible to criticise an author's work adequately until you have understood what kind of books he was writing.'[3] *Homage to Catalonia* (1938), which contains autobiography, military history, political analysis and propaganda, is problematical in this respect and seems a mixture of 'kinds', for the structure of the book is determined by Orwell's motivations and psychological needs as well as by the pattern of historical events. The *genre* of *Homage* is war memoir and its model those classic accounts of the Great War, narrated from the victim's viewpoint, which Orwell discusses in 'Inside the Whale'. Hugh Thomas, writing from a historian's viewpoint, warns that Orwell's account 'should be read with reservations. It is more accurate about war itself than about the Spanish War.'[4] This statement emphasizes Orwell's affinity to the novelists of the Great War and also suggests that he wrote his best books about real, and not fictional, experience.

Critics have frequently noted that Orwell's war experience in Spain provided the original impetus for his late political satires, but they have not observed that *Homage* is closely related to his early life and personal narratives, and that its central theme of comradeship and human solidarity, the main support of the victim in war, is an expression of his intense need to be accepted by and 'involved in mankind'. *Homage* is written with the directness and immediacy of a personal vision, and portrays not only an eye-witness account of what happened in Spain, but also the story of a man's growth in personal and political awareness. The central tension between politics and war, reflection and action, disenchantment and idealism, creates the dominatn form of *Homage* and reflects the poignant opposition of victimization and comradeship.

In 'Why I Write', Orwell states that '*Homage to Catalonia* is, of course, a frankly political book, but in the main it is written with a certain detachment and regard for form. I did try very hard in it to tell the whole truth without violating my literary instincts' (1.6). Though critics find the political chapters merely ephemeral and obstructive, Orwell's evaluation is reliable and his creative instinct sound. The form of the book, which he said was 'the best I have written' (III.392), is finely wrought.

The structure of *Homage* is based on two contrasts. First, the descriptions of combat on the Aragon front are contrasted to Orwell's three visits to Barcelona in December, April and June. Second, at each visit the revolution has rapidly deteriorated, so that the radically reversed political conditions provide an increasingly dramatic and ironic reflection on his previous stay. Orwell's two apparently distinct purposes converge and unify as the four dominant events of the book reveal that the military action at the front is negated by the political events in Barcelona. The parapet attack (chapter 7) and Orwell's wound (chapter 12) climax his two visits to the front; the fighting around the Café Moka (chapter 10) and his attempt to rescue Kopp (chapter 14) climax his two returns to Barcelona.

The book opens in December 1936 as Orwell enlists in the militia and experiences for the first time the 'special atmosphere' of revolutionary spirit in Barcelona.[5] After the briefest and most ineffectual 'training', he is sent to the front in early January, and remains there until the parapet attack. He returns to Barcelona on 26 April to find that the Civil War has become triangular, with the Communists and Socialists fighting each other as well'as the Fascists, and spends most of his leave involved in street-fighting for the Socialists. He returns to the front on 10 May, disillusioned though awakened, and is shot through the throat ten days later. He spends the next month first in various hospitals and then seeking his discharge papers, and returns to Barcelona for the last time on 20 June to discover his militia-party outlawed and his life in danger. Though pursued by the police, he attempts to rescue his *Commandante*, Georges Kopp, and barely escapes to France on 23 June.

The political chapters, like chapter 8 and the end of chapter 14, are reflective and establish an effective contrast to the action. These chapters serve as interludes which place Orwell's experiences in perspective: chapter 5 separates the five chapters on the Aragon front (2–4, 6–7) and explains the stalemate that has been described in the earlier chapters (the Loyalist armies are divided and cannot mount and sustain an offensive); chapter 11 explains the reasons for the street-fighting narrated in the previous chapter. Though the subject of *Homage* is war, Orwell insists 'it would be quite impossible to write about the Spanish War from a purely military angle. It was above all things a political war.'[6] The vital connection between personal narration and political reporting of the war is skilfully emphasized by the description of his retreat from the parapet and retreat from the Hotel Continental, where the police are searching for him. Both events are narrated in brief staccato dialogue: the repetition of a curt but urgent command and a puzzled response by Orwell – 'Get out of it!' 'Why?' and 'Get out of here *at once*!' 'What?' – are followed by his halting movement in the ordered direction.

The political and military atmosphere of *Homage* resembles the chaotic conditions of *Nostromo*, in which history is nothing more than

> stories of political outrage; friends, relatives, ruined, imprisoned, killed in the battles of senseless civil wars, barbarously executed in ferocious proscriptions. . . . Oppression, inefficiency, fatuous methods, treachery, and savage brutality [ruled].[7]

As Bernanos writes of his painful Civil War experiences:

> The tragedy of Spain is a foretaste of the tragedy of the universe. It is the shattering proof of the unhappy condition of men of good will in modern society, which little by little eliminates them, as a by-product that can be turned to no good account.[8]

These 'men of good will' are always the victims of war, and it is from this traditional viewpoint that Orwell narrates his war memoir. He specifically compares the Spanish to the Great War – 'It was a bad copy of 1914–18, a positional war of trenches, artillery, raids, snipers, mud, barbed wire, lice and stagnation' (1.538) – and defines his tradition by comparing books on both wars. In 'Inside the Whale' (1940), Orwell criticizes the Spanish war books for 'their shocking dullness and badness', and states that 'almost all of them, right-wing or left-wing, are written from a political angle, by cocksure partisans telling you what to think'. *Homage to Catalonia*, on the other hand, is distinguished from these books by its truthfulness and objectivity, and by its frank portrayal of Orwell's helplessness and confusion. Though more polemical and positive than books about the Great War, *Homage* belongs in that tradition because of its sensitive portrayal of a sympathetic and helpless victim. For those books were also

> written by common soldiers or junior officers who did not even pretend to understand what the whole thing was about. Books like *All Quiet on the Western Front, Le Feu, A Farewell to Arms, Death of a Hero, Good-Bye to All That, Memoirs of an Infantry Officer* and *A Subaltern on the Somme* were written not by propagandists but by *victims*.[9] They are saying, in effect, 'What the hell is this about? God knows. All we can do is to endure.' . . . They are the records of something completely meaningless, a nightmare happening in a void. That was not actually the truth about the war, but it was the truth about the individual reaction. The soldier advancing into a machine-gun barrage or standing waist-deep in a flooded trench knew only that here was an appalling experience in which he was all but helpless. He was likelier to make a good book out of his helplessness and his ignorance than out of a pretended power to see the whole thing in perspective. (1.501, 523–4)

Orwell's achievement was to create a meaningful work out of his immediate involvement in a contemporary event, despite his limited perspective and political ignorance, and his book still stands as the most valuable English account of the Spanish war.

In squalid misery and unspeakable horror, Orwell's experiences on the Aragon front surpassed anything he had previously endured in Burma[10] or Wigan or while 'down and out'. He insists that, in war, 'the physical details always outweigh everything else', and he is constantly submerged in an atmosphere of 'filth and chaos', 'excrement and decay', 'boredom and discomfort' – in 'mud, lice, hunger, cold'. The 'nightmare' feeling is constantly stressed, and rats appear frequently. During the parapet attack he feels 'a deep horror at everything: the chaos, the darkness, the frightful din, the slithering to and fro in the mud'. When he is wounded, he finds the medical treatment almost as crude as in the days of Hogarth and Smollett. When he returns to Barcelona, he finds the suspicion and hostility of his former comrades 'sickening and disillusioning'.[11]

For Orwell, helpless and confused, war is a trial by ordeal that ends with his wound and his flight. The most interesting things about his narrative are his startling honesty and the accuracy of his psychological responses. Orwell admits that he is often frightened: when going to the front, the first time under fire and especially after his wound, when he loses his nerve completely. He confesses that he is ineffectual in combat, deceived in a crisis, absurd as a smuggler, self-indulgent on leave. Yet this seems to generalize his experiences (we would be the same) and to engage our sympathies as he becomes a kind of military archetype who embodies 'the fate of most soldiers in most wars'. Though a soldier, he is always a sensitive humanist, who observes, 'It was the first time in my life that I had fired a gun at a human being.' When he is under fire he reacts with instinctive and futile gestures: he ducks, he claps his hand over his cheek, 'as though one's hand could stop a bullet! – but I had a horror of being hit in the face'. Instead, he is shot through the neck and, like Joyce Cary, who was wounded in the German Cameroons in 1915, manages a detached and 'posthumous' reflection in the midst of the horrible experience. Cary states:

> I got a bullet that scraped my mastoid, and of course it felt as if my brains were blown to pieces, and it knocked me right out. And I just sat down to think: 'Well this is it, and it is easy.'[12]

Similarly, Orwell observes:

> Roughly speaking it was the sensation of being *at the centre* of an explosion. There seemed to be a loud bang and a blinding flash of light all round me, and I felt a tremendous shock – no pain, only a violent shock, such as you get from an electric terminal; with it a sense of utter weakness, a feeling of being stricken and shrivelled up to nothing. . . . I knew immediately that I was hit, but because of the seeming bang and flash I thought it was a rifle nearby that had gone off accidentally and shot me. All this happened in a space of time much less than a second. The

next moment my knees crumpled up and I was falling, my head hitting the ground with a violent bang which, to my relief, did not hurt. I had a numb, dazed feeling, a consciousness of being very badly hurt, but no pain in the ordinary sense.[13]

Though Orwell's vivid account is a re-created experience, it conveys the illusion of immediacy by a subjective series of closely observed details – the bang, the flash, the shock. These are followed by a more objective analysis of what happened, a concentration on his fall instead of his wound, and a grateful relief about pain that indirectly verifies his survival.

Orwell's wound is carefully complemented by those of his wounded comrades, a procession of ghastly, bloody, lonely creatures, who pass through the book like figures from Goya's *Disasters of War* and evoke Orwell's pity and sympathy:

There was one man wounded in the face and throat who had his head inside a sort of spherical helmet of butter-muslin. . . . He looked so lonely, wandering to and fro.

There was a roar of the explosion and then, instantly, a diabolical outcry of screams and groans. . . . Poor wretch! I felt a vague sorrow as I heard him screaming.

The 'vague sorrow' is a sensitive insight that subtly suggests the enormous differences between the healthy and the wounded. When the injured men are sent back to the hospitals, the ambulances file down the abominable road to Sietamo, flinging the soldiers from their stretchers and killing the badly wounded with their joltings; and when Orwell is shot he endures the horrors of the same ride: 'No one who was liable to bleed internally could have survived those miles of jolting.' The tender pity in these passages is reminiscent of 'How the Poor Die'.

Strangely enough, war, for Orwell, is not all futility and suffering. He reverts at times to the self-conscious and adventurous Boy Scout attitude of the Eton OTC, where sniping and whizzing bullets are 'rather fun', patrols and trenches are 'not bad fun in a way', and building barricades is 'a strange and wonderful sight'. Here the boyish naïveté in combat, a kind of playful whistling in the dark, is the military correlative of Orwell's political innocence. But as the political realities darken his vision,the fighting does not seem quite so much 'fun' as before.[14] In a crucial way, *Homage* is a *Bildungsroman der Realpolitik*, for Orwell moves a great distance from

> [the fall of Málaga] set up in my mind the first vague doubts about this war in which, hitherto, the rights and wrongs had seemed so beautifully simple,

to

> The fact is that every war suffers a kind of progressive degradation with every month that it continues, because such things as individual liberty and a truthful press are simply not compatible with military efficiency.

Like all victims in war, Orwell is immersed in immediate events and confused about the political situation, and in the book his perspective is not clarified until his political awareness gradually develops. 'There is no such thing as a genuinely non-political literature,' writes Orwell in 1946, 'and least of all in an age like our own, when fears, hatreds and loyalties of a directly political kind are near to the surface of everyone's consciousness' (IV.65). And, he adds in the same year, a writer's 'subject matter will be determined by the age he lives in' (I.3). Orwell believes that one of the primary obligations of the writer is to be honest, to establish the truth; and he writes of *Homage*, 'I happened to know, what very few people in England had been allowed to know, that innocent men were being falsely accused. If I had not been angry about that I should never have written the book' (I.6).

Orwell came to know this truth by a series of accidents. He describes his connection with POUM, 'the most extreme of the revolutionary parties' (I.287), in 'Notes on the Spanish Militias':

> Just before leaving England I rang up the ILP, with which I had some slight connections, mainly personal, and asked them to give me some kind of recommendation. They sent me a letter . . . to John McNair at Barcelona. . . . [I] produced my letter to McNair (whom I did not know) and through this I joined the POUM militia. . . . At that time I was only

> rather dimly aware of the differences between the political parties. ....
> Had I a complete understanding of the situation I should have probably
> joined the CNT militia. (1.318)[15]

Hugh Thomas writes of POUM that

> Many joined this party believing that it represented a mean between the
> indiscipline of the Anarchists and the strictness of the PSUC [Socialists].
> Foreigners in Barcelona joined the POUM in the romantic supposition
> that it indeed embodied a magnificent Utopian aspiration.[16]

Though Orwell idealistically affirms, 'There are occasions when
it pays better to fight and be beaten than not to fight at all,'[17] he
also states: 'As a militiaman one was a soldier against Franco, but
one was also a pawn in an enormous struggle that was being fought
out between two political theories.' For, as Orwell gradually
recognizes, the real struggle is between revolution and counter-
revolution, between the Comintern and the Spanish left-wing
parties. The Russian government tried to prevent revolution in
Spain, just as it had done in China ten years earlier.[18]

The retrogression of Barcelona from a revolutionary to a bourgeois to a totalitarian city is paralleled by the decline of the POUM
party. First, writes Orwell, it

> was an accepted party and supplied a minister to the Catalan Government;
> later it was expelled from the Government; then it was denounced as
> Trotskyist; then it was suppressed, every member that the police could
> lay their hands on being flung in jail. (1.274)

Trotsky in Russia, Snowball in *Animal Farm*, suffered a similar fate.

There is considerable confusion in *Homage* (Orwell tells what
happens, but not *why*), because he, like everyone else, did not
understand why the Communists destroyed their Socialist allies.[19]
And his bewilderment continued beyond 1943, when he said, 'As
to the Russians, their motives in the Spanish war are completely
inscrutable' (11.263). This confusion results because the Russian policy
was both contradictory and ineffectual. As Isaac Deutscher writes,

> Stalin's desire [was] to preserve for the Spanish Popular Front its repub-
> lican respectability and to avoid antagonizing the British and French

Governments. He saved nobody's respectability and he antagonized everybody. Conservative opinion in the west, not interested in the internecine struggle of the Spanish left and confused by the intricacies of Stalin's policy, blamed Stalin as the chief fomenter of revolution.[20]

According to Orwell, 'The sin of nearly all left-wingers from 1933 onwards is that they have wanted to be anti-Fascist without being anti-totalitarian' (III.236). They tolerated and even endorsed Stalin because he fought against the Fascists, though both sides used the same brutal methods. Except for Orwell, Trotsky, Borkenau and a few others, no one seemed to realize 'that among the parties on the Government side the Communists stood not upon the extreme Left, but upon the extreme Right'. Since the Loyalist revolutionaries had no footing in the foreign press, Orwell had to tell the truth. But he was a voice crying in the wilderness: his book sold only six hundred copies in its first twelve years, and was not even published in America until after his death.

For Orwell, this Loyalist internecine strife was more horrible than actual warfare against the Fascists. During the street-fighting, 'I was in no danger, I suffered from nothing worse than hunger and boredom, yet it was one of the most unbearable periods in my whole life. I think few experiences could be more sickening, more disillusioning or, finally, more nerve-racking.' Yet Orwell's 'thrill of hope' was never extinguished and he remained 'an affirming flame':

> Whenever you have had a glimpse of such a disaster as this – and however it ends the Spanish war will turn out to have been an appalling disaster, quite apart from the slaughter and the physical suffering – the result is not necessarily disillusionment and cynicism. Curiously enough the whole experience has left me with not less but more belief in the decency of human beings.

His conception of human decency is manifested in comradeship and solidarity, and is symbolized by the moving handshakes of the Italian militiaman and the Spanish police officer at the beginning and end of the book. This idea of comradeship is at the very core of *Homage* and is elaborated in numerous ways – humanistic, psychological, idealistic and heroic. For Orwell shares the concept of 'the virile fraternity' with the great masculine writers like Melville, Conrad, and Malraux, who writes of Vincent Berger in *The Walnut Trees of Altenburg*: 'What he liked about war was the masculine comradeship, the irrevocable commitments that courage imposes.'[21] This sense of a brotherhood that shares the intimacy of death is general rather than local and extends to all combatants. When enemy deserters slip across the Loyalist lines and Orwell sees his first 'real Fascists', 'It struck me that they were indistinguishable from ourselves, except that they wore khaki overalls.' And when he lies next to a wounded Assault Guard in Monzon Hospital, he says, 'In Barcelona we should have been shooting one another,' and they laugh over this. Similarly, during the soldiers' talk across the rooftop barricades near the Café Moka (which recalls the famous scene in *The Red Badge of Courage* where foes converse along a narrow river bank), the peaceful Orwell yells:

> 'Hi! Don't you shoot at us!'
> 'What?'
> 'Don't you fire at us or we'll fire back!'
> 'No, No! I wasn't firing at you. . . . We don't want to shoot you. We are only workers, the same as you are.'

This powerful bond makes Orwell a reluctant warrior. Once, in the trenches, Orwell suddenly came very close to an enemy and 'could see him clearly. He was bareheaded and seemed to have nothing on except a blanket which he was clutching round his shoulders. If I had fired I could have blown him to pieces. . . . [but] I never even thought of firing.' Instead, Orwell chases him and prods him with a bayonet but never quite catches him – 'a comic memory for me to look back upon, though I suppose it seemed less comic to him'. The point here is that Orwell does not really want to kill the man, and this is reinforced by the well-known incident described in ' Looking Back on the Spanish War' (1943). Again, a vulnerable enemy suddenly appears:

> He was half-dressed and was holding up his trousers with both hands as he ran. I refrained from shooting at him. . . . I had come here to shoot at

'Fascists'; but a man who is holding up his trousers isn't a 'Fascist', he is visibly a fellow creature, similar to yourself, and you don't feel like shooting at him. (II.254)[22]

This sense of comradeship and solidarity that Orwell experienced in Spain answered his deep-rooted psychological need. We have seen that at school and in Burma, Paris, London and Wigan, Orwell had been a lonely outsider, and that this feeling of intense isolation is reflected in his fictional heroes – Flory, Dorothy and Comstock. He took his wife to Spain right after their marriage, and it was the first time in his life that he was not isolated and alien. United in a common cause with the Spanish Loyalists, he became passionately attached to them.

Orwell's powerful sense of solidarity in Spain is related to the symbolic experience in Wigan when he overcomes his fears, enters a common lodging-house, and is initiated by a drunken stevedore who cries, ' 'Ave a cup of tea, chum!' He writes that this moment 'was a kind of baptism ... everybody was polite and gentle and took me utterly for granted. ... [I was] on terms of utter equality with working-class people.'[23] If tramp life is Orwell's 'baptism', life in the Spanish militia is his 'confirmation' – in true equality and comradeship with the working class for the first time in his life. For in Aragon they were

all living at the same level and mingling on terms of equality. ... One had been in contact with something strange and valuable. One had been in a community where hope was more normal than apathy or cynicism, where the word 'comrade' stood for comradeship. ... One had breathed the air of equality. ... [This period] is now of great importance to me. It is so different from the rest of my life.

The stevedore's momentous acceptance of Orwell is repeated in another moving, almost ceremonial incident, concerning the dark ragged boy in his section who was accused of stealing, stripped naked and then exonerated. Orwell believed him guilty and was ashamed of his humiliation. Shortly afterwards, when Corporal Orwell got into a dispute with his men about the need for discipline, this boy sprang into the ring and began passionately defending me. With his strange, wild, Indian gesture he kept exclaiming, 'He's the best corporal we've got'. . . . Why is this incident touching to me? Because in any normal circumstances it would have been impossible for good feelings ever to be re-established between this boy and myself. (II.255)

Besides Orwell's constant affirmation of the value of the individual in the midst of degradation, there are other striking parallels between the 'down and out' period and Spain. For *Homage*, as Orwell says, is a focal point in his career: it both epitomizes his earlier experiences among the poor and oppressed and foreshadows his political satires. When he first became attracted to the poor he had 'no interest in Socialism or any other economic theory',[24] and when he first came to Catalonia he 'ignored the political side of the war'. He states in *Wigan Pier* that he wanted to side with the oppressed against their tyrants; and the ex-police officer repeats in *Homage*, 'when I see an actual flesh-and-blood worker in conflict with his natural enemy, the policeman, I do not have to ask myself which side I am on'. Because the Trotskyist POUM party was the defeated faction of the defeated side, it was deeply attractive to Orwell, and answered his need to seek failure and to become a victim. He loved the hopeless individuality of the undisciplined and ill-armed militia, partly because it made military life more difficult and dangerous.

Orwell feels that fighting in the militia, like his life with the tramps, is both exciting and dull : 'it was simply the mingled boredom and discomfort of stationary warfare . . .[but] it was rather fun wandering about the dark valleys with stray bullets flying high overhead.' And like his encounter with the Wigan miners, his friendship with the Italian militiaman, who symbolizes the best qualities of the European working class, transcends class differences for an ephemeral solidarity and comradeship:

I liked them and hoped they liked me; but I went among them as a foreigner, and both of us were aware of it. (*Wigan Pier*)

It was as though his spirit and mine had momentarily succeeded in bridging the gulf of language and tradition and meeting in utter intimacy. I hope he liked me as well as I liked him. (*Homage*)

Orwell confesses he hardly knows why he took such an 'immediate liking' to the militiaman, and his powerful attraction to the commonplace youth remains vague. More symbolic than real, he exists as a prototype of a soldier-hero and embodiment of the 'special atmosphere' of the time (the 'palms are only able/ To meet within the sound of guns,' II.266). Orwell idealizes this man in the same way he did the Burmese, tramps and miners; and Boxer, in *Animal Farm*, is an equine version of the illiterate Italian.

The 'special atmosphere' that Orwell describes is one where the primary emotions are released, a time of generous feelings and humane gestures. It is also a time that reveals the very roots of human solidarity, for 'war brings it home to the individual that he is *not* altogether an individual' (II.94). This comradeship, so vital and so necessary to Orwell, begins even before he reaches Spain, for the night he leaves Paris, the slow train 'was packed with Czechs, Germans, Frenchmen, all bound on the same mission'. The male pyramid that the sleeping volunteers form on the floor of the train foreshadows Orwell's vivid memory of 'young Ramón snoring with his nose flattened between my shoulder-blades'. And when they wake in the morning, the French peasants in the fields 'stood solemnly upright and gave the anti-Fascist salute' (III.232).[25] The political implications of these symbolic incidents is clear: though the international working class achieves solidarity in time of war, they are destined to defeat. This, for Orwell, is perhaps the great tragedy of the inter-war period, from the assassination of Rosa Luxemburg and Karl Liebknecht to the paralysis of the Labour Party when confronted with Spain and with Munich.[26]

But the militiaman is also a sacrificial victim, martyred by lies and treacherous guns, and forgotten 'before your bones were dry'. In this respect his fate is like the meaningless death in a Spanish jail of Bob Smillie, the son of the labour leader, who had been on the French train with Orwell and had fought with courage and willingness, and the cruel and absurd imprisonment of Orwell's hero in the book, Georges Kopp.

This brave Belgian, who is first seen riding a black horse at the head of a column, represents the ideal military leader and reappears at the moments of intense crisis and action – at the parapet assault, the Café Moka attack and the POUM purge in Barcelona. He calls the stagnant trench warfare 'a comic opera with an occasional death'; and during the chaotic street-fighting, walks 'unarmed up to men who were frightened out of their wits and had loaded guns in their hands' in order to prevent bloodshed. After Kopp's arrest, Orwell gives a proud resumé of his life and character:

> He was a man who had sacrificed everything – family, nationality, liveli-
> hood – simply to come to Spain and fight against Fascism. . . . He had
> piled up years of imprisonment for himself if he should ever return to his
> own country. He had been in the line since October 1936, had worked
> his way up from militiaman to major, had been in action I do not know
> how many times, and had been wounded once.

Orwell's courageous attempt to rescue Kopp is a failure, and he flees Spain believing his friend will be shot. But the publication of Orwell's letters reveals that in December 1938 Kopp escaped to England 'after 18 months in a GPU jail, in which he lost seven stone of weight' (1.370).[27] Kopp continued his amazing career, for Orwell's editors write,

> He joined the French Foreign Legion in September 1939 and was
> captured by the Germans . . . in June 1940. He escaped from a French
> military hospital and worked . . . for British Naval Intelligence until
> betrayed to the Gestapo. (1. 263n)

Kopp was rescued by the British in 1943 and died from war wounds in 1951.

Orwell's own 'anti-heroic' character is the opposite of Kopp's, who represents an ideal standard against which Orwell measures his own inadequate self. Two of Orwell's contrasting but related roles are presented in the book: comrade and victim. His belief in comradeship allows him to be exploited, and this victimization re-affirms, ironically, his idealistic belief in the 'virile fraternity'.

Spain itself, as a concept and a reality,[28] inspired idealism. Orwell had, as we have seen in *Wigan Pier*, a deep desire to expiate his childhood and imperialistic guilt by joining the oppressed and experiencing degradation. He needed to do this, not only for the Baudelairean sense of self-mortification, but also to experience the spiritual triumph of preserving decency by a compassionate suffering for others. According to Stephen Spender, who observed the War as a non-combatant,

> within a few weeks Spain had become the symbol of hope for all anti-Fascists. It offered the twentieth century an 1848: that is to say, a time and place where a cause representing a greater degree of freedom and justice than a reactionary one, gained victories. It became possible to see the Fascist–anti-Fascist struggle as a real conflict of ideas, not just as the seizure of powers by dictators from weak opponents. From being a pathetic catastrophe, Spain lifted the fate of the anti-Fascists to the heights of tragedy.[29]

And Orwell confirms these exalted feelings when he writes soon after his return to England, 'No one who was in Spain during the months when people still believed in the revolution will ever forget that strange and moving experience' (1.287). Four years later he states that the Spanish 'civil war made a deep and painful impression on the English intelligentsia, deeper, I should say, than has yet been made by the war now raging'.[30] And in his review of Borkenau's *The Spanish Cockpit*, he echoes Kipling's 'Tommy' and refers to the International Brigade as 'a thin line of suffering and often ill-armed human beings standing between barbarism and at least comparative decency' (1.278).

Orwell was always volunteering for the most difficult and dangerous missions; and when he found things too quiet in Aragon, he tried to join the International Brigade and get sent into combat at the Madrid front. He first came to Spain as a journalist but 'joined the militia almost immediately, because at that time and in that atmosphere it seemed the only conceivable thing to do'. He volunteers for the parapet attack and to recover the wounded afterward, and to smuggle rifles back to the POUM building. And he offers himself in Sietamo when it appears that fighting will start again, although he has a hole in his neck and a medical discharge and is too weak to jump down from the lorry. Far more than most men, Orwell lived his words: 'To understand a political movement one has got to be involved in it' (1.348). The greatness of *Homage to Catalonia* is that Orwell's idealism and courage are embodied in his spirit and action.

Just after he returned to England from Spain, Orwell wrote with some bitterness that 'We started off by being heroic defenders of democracy and ended by slipping over the border with the police panting on our heels' (1.279). Just as his moving description of life in the Spanish militia (a 'forecast of what the opening stages of Socialism might be like') is similar in feeling to the joyous though short-lived freedom of Animal Farm after the Rebellion, so his hostility to the Russian Communists was a direct result of the betrayal in Spain.

Though *Homage* was largely ignored and Orwell's attempt to communicate the terrible truths he discovered in Spain was a practical failure, he felt compelled to stimulate his countrymen into political awareness. As he writes in the Preface to *Animal Farm*: 'Up to 1939, and even later, the majority of English people were incapable of assessing the true nature of the Nazi régime in Germany, and now, with the Soviet régime, they are still to a large extent under the same sort of illusion. . . . It was of the utmost importance to me that people in western Europe should see the Soviet régime for what it really was' (III.404–5). When he published the immensely popular *Animal Farm* in 1945, Orwell was able to communicate these insights not only to Europe, but to the entire world.

> The worker in his human functions no longer
> feels himself to be anything but animal. What is
> animal becomes human and what is human
> becomes animal.
>
> KARL MARX, *Economic and*
> *Philosophic Manuscripts of 1844*

ORWELL BELIEVES THAT 'The business of making people *conscious* of what is happening outside their own small circle is one of the major problems of our time, and a new literary technique will have to be evolved to meet it' (IV.270). His choice of a satiric beast fable for *Animal Farm* (1945) was exactly what he needed, for his creation of characters was always rather weak, and the flat symbolic animals of the fable did not have to be portrayed in depth. The familiar and affectionate tone of the story and its careful attention to detail allowed the unpopular theme to be pleasantly convincing, and the Soviet myth was exposed in a subtle fashion that could still be readily understood. It was written in clear and simple language that could be easily translated, and was short so that it could be sold cheaply and read quickly. The gay *genre* was a final attempt to deflect his profound pessimism, which dominated his final realistic vision of decency trampled on and destroyed in *1984*.

Experimentation with the literary techniques that could most forcefully convey his ideas is characteristic of all Orwell's non-fiction: autobiographical, sociological, and political. Though he had considerable success as a polemicist and pamphleteer, this *genre* was too blunt and too direct, for his views were extremely unpopular at the time he expressed them. *Animal Farm* was written between November 1943 and February 1944, after Stalingrad and before

Normandy, when the Allies first became victorious and there was a strong feeling of solidarity with the Russians, who even in retreat had deflected Hitler from England. Distinguished writers like Wells, Shaw, Barbusse and Rolland had praised Russia highly. But Orwell's book belongs with Trotsky's *The Revolution Betrayed* (1937),[1] Gide's *Return From the U.S.S.R.* (1937) and Koestler's *Darkness At Noon* (1941), three prescient attacks on the Stalinist régime; and it anticipates post-war denunciations like Crossman's compilation *The God That Failed* (1949) and Djilas' *The New Class* (1957).

Orwell had defined the theme of this book as early as 'Inside the Whale' (1940); and he writes in his essay on James Burnham (1946), 'History consists of a series of swindles, in which the masses are first lured into revolt by the promise of Utopia, and then, when they have done their job, enslaved over again by new masters' (IV.177). In his Preface to the Ukrainian edition of *Animal Farm* (1947), he states that

> The man-hunts in Spain went on at the same time as the great purges in the USSR and were a sort of supplement to them. . . . Nothing has contributed so much to the corruption of the original idea of Socialism as the belief that Russia is a Socialist country and that every act of its rulers must be excused, if not imitated. And so for the past ten years I have been convinced that the destruction of the Soviet myth was essential if we wanted a revival of the Socialist movement. (III.404–5)

Orwell fused his artistic and political purpose so well that the animals are completely convincing on the literal level. His precise portrayal of the beasts is based on his practical experience as a farmer at Wallington, where he lived from 1936 to 1940 (and kept a goat called Muriel). Though critics emphasize his statement, 'Most of the good memories of my childhood . . . are in some way connected with animals' (IV.345), the most important animals in the story, the pigs (and their dogs), are frightening and ferocious. Orwell utilizes the repulsive associations of Circean and Gadarene swine that have prevailed since ancient times,[2] and was undoubtedly influenced by the talking horses in Book IV of *Gulliver's Travels*. Yahoos slave

for Houyhnhnms as animals do for pigs; and horses 'milk their
Cows, and reap their Oats, and do all the work which requires
Hands'[3] just as 'the pigs sent for buckets and milked the cows fairly
successfully, their trotters being well-adapted to this task'.[4] Orwell
seems to dislike pigs, for in *Coming Up For Air*, Bowling is frightened by

> a herd of pigs [that] was galloping, a sort of huge flood of pig-faces.
> The next moment, of course, I saw what it was. It wasn't pig faces at all,
> it was only schoolchildren in their gas-masks. . . . But I tell you that for a
> moment they looked exactly like a herd of pigs.[5]

This hostility continued after the success of *Animal Farm*, and he
writes from Jura in 1948, 'I have tried the experiment of keeping a
pig. They really are disgusting brutes. . . . The pig has grown to a
stupendous size and goes to the butcher next week. We are all
longing to get rid of him, as he is so destructive and greedy, even
gets into the kitchen sometimes' (iv.451, 458).

Like the American publisher who rejected *Animal Farm* because
'it was impossible to sell animal stories in the USA' (iv.110),
critics have been deceived and disarmed by the apparent simplicity
of this 'fairy story'. Atkins writes in 1954, 'In his revaluation of
Animal Farm in *World Review* (June 1950) Tom Hopkinson says
that this novel is one of the two modern works of fiction before
which the critic must abdicate. . . . There is so much truth in this that
I find it very difficult to say anything useful about the book and yet
a study of Orwell cannot ignore it altogether.'[6] Two years later
Hollis concurs that 'The story of *Animal Farm* is so familiar that
it hardly needs detailed recapitulation. . . . The interpretation of the
fable is plain enough. . . . As I say, there is no difficulty in inter-
preting the symbolism of the story.'[7] In 1962 Rees agrees, '*Animal
Farm* is so well known that it cannot be necessary to do more than
mention some of its major felicities';[8] and Thomas repeats three
years later, 'The story is too well-known for anything but a brief
summary to be given here.'[9] And the next year Woodcock reaffirms
that Orwell 'produced a book so clear in intent and writing that

the critic is usually rather nonplussed as to what he should say about it; all is so magnificently there'.[10] Though critics have often interpreted the book in terms of Soviet history, they have never sufficiently recognized that it is extremely subtle and sophisticated, and brilliantly presents a satiric allegory of Communist Russia in which virtually every detail has political significance.

Orwell describes the creative impulse of the book in his Preface:

> I saw a little boy, perhaps ten years old, driving a huge cart-horse along a narrow path, whipping it whenever it tried to turn. It struck me that if only such animals became aware of their strength we should have no power over them, and that men exploit animals in much the same way as the rich exploit the proletariat. I proceeded to analyse Marx's theory from the animals' point of view. (III.405–6)

Major's speech is an accurate exposition of orthodox Marxism and is very similar to the last paragraph of the *Communist Manifesto* (1848):[11] the Communists

> openly declare that their ends can be attained only by the forcible overthrow of all existing social conditions. Let the ruling classes tremble at the Communistic revolution. The proletarians have nothing to lose but their chains. They have a world to win. WORKINGMEN OF ALL COUNTRIES, UNITE![12]

In his *Critique of the Gotha Program*, Marx stated, 'From each according to his abilities, to each according to his needs'; and when Animal Farm is established, 'everyone worked according to his capacity'. And Squealer's ingenious gloss on 'Four legs good, two legs bad' is a witty and ironic example of specious Marxist polemics: 'A bird's wing, comrades . . . is an organ of propulsion and not of manipulation. It should therefore be regarded as a leg.'

'Comrade Napoleon', the poem of Minimus (who is based on the poet Mayakovsky)[13] is a close imitation of adulatory Soviet verse like the 'Hymn to J. V. Stalin':

> The world has no person
> Dearer, closer,
> With him, happiness is happier,
> And the sun brighter.[14]

Friend of the fatherless!
Fountain of happiness!
Lord of the swill-bucket! Oh, how my soul is on
Fire when I gaze at thy
Calm and commanding eye,
Like the sun in the sky,
Comrade Napoleon!

And parts of the revolutionary song, 'Beasts of England', closely paraphrase certain lines of 'L'Internationale' (1871):

C'est l'éruption de la fin
Soon or late the day is coming

Paix entre nous, guerre aux tyrans!
Tyrant Man shall be o'erthrown

La terre n'appartient qu'aux hommes
And the fruitful fields of England
Shall be trod by beasts alone.

Foule esclave, debout! Debout!
Rings shall vanish from our noses

Le soleil brillera toujours!
Bright will shine the fields of England.

'L'Internationale' expresses the brief but idealistic exhilaration that Orwell experienced under the short-lived Anarchist government in Barcelona. As he wrote to Cyril Connolly from Spain in 1937, 'I have seen wonderful things & at last really believe in Socialism, which I never did before' (1.269).

Immediately after the pigs celebrate their victory and bury 'some hams hanging in the kitchen' (a wonderful detail), the revolutionary principles of Major are codified by Snowball into 'The Seven Commandments' (which are reminiscent of the Five Chief Beatitudes of the Pukka Sahib in Burmese Days). The corruption inherent in the Rebellion is manifested as each of the Commandments is successively betrayed, until none of the original revolutionary idealism remains. As in Orwell's early novels and 1984, the structure of the book is circular, and by the time the name is changed back to Manor Farm, there has been a return to the *status quo* (or worse) with whisky and whips in the trotters of the pigs.

In the Preface to *Animal Farm*, Orwell writes: 'Although various episodes are taken from the actual history of the Russian Revolution, they are dealt with schematically and their chronological order is changed' (III.406). Thus, the human beings are capitalists, the animals are Communists, the wild creatures who could not be tamed and 'continued to behave very much as before' are the *muzhiks* or peasants, the pigs are the Bolsheviks, the Rebellion is the October Revolution, the neighbouring farmers are the western armies who attempted to support the Czarists against the Reds, the wave of rebelliousness that ran through the countryside afterwards is the abortive revolutions in Hungary and Germany in 1919 and 1923, the hoof and horn is the hammer and sickle, the Spontaneous Demonstration is the May Day celebration, the Order of the Green Banner is the Order of Lenin, the special pig committee presided over by Napoelon is the Politbureau, the revolt of the hens – the *first* rebellion since the expulsion of Jones (the Czar) – is the sailors' rebellion at the Kronstadt naval base in 1921, and Napoleon's dealings with Whymper and the Willingdon markets represent the Treaty of Rapallo, signed with Germany in 1922, which ended the capitalists' boycott of Soviet Russia.

The carefully chosen names are both realistic and highly suggestive of their owners' personalities and roles in the fable. The imperious Major (Marx-Lenin) is military, dominant and senior (in public school jargon); the rather stupid and self-sacrificing Boxer (the proletariat), who is contrasted to the cynical Benjamin and the indifferent and unenthusiastic cat, is named after the Chinese revolutionaries who drove out foreign exploiters and were themselves crushed; Mollie (the White Russians) suggests folly, and her retrogressive defection for vanity and luxury is a paradigm of the entire revolution; Moses (the Russian Orthodox and later the Catholic Church) brings divine law to man; Squealer (a living *Pravda*) is onomatopoetic for a voluble pig; and Whymper, the pigs' agent, suggests a toady. Pilkington (Churchill–England), the capitalist exploiter, connotes 'bilk' and 'milk' (slang): he is an old-fashioned gentleman who enjoys country sports on Foxwood, which has associations of both craftiness and the Tory landed gentry. Frederick (Hitler) refers to Frederick the Great, the founder of the Prussian military state and Hitler's hero. Frederick is a tough, shrewd man who drives hard bargains, steals other people's land for his own farm, Pinchfield, and practices terrible cruelites upon his subjects. These cruelties are related to the most moving scene in the novel – when Boxer is taken to the slaughter-house – for the knacker's van recalls the terrible gas vans used by the *Einsatzgruppen* for mobile extermination. Though Clover screams out, 'They are taking you to your death,' the sound of Boxer's drumming hoofs inside the van 'grew fainter and died away'.

The most important animals are Napoleon (Stalin) and Snowball (Trotsky), whose personalities are antithetical and who are never in agreement. Both characters are drawn fully and accurately, though with simple strokes, and reflect almost all the dominant characteristics of their historical models. Like Trotsky, Orwell compares Stalin to Napoleon, for both turned revolutions into dictatorships (Bona-partism was the successor to Thermidor), both transformed a national popular 'revolution from below' into a foreign conqueror's 'revolution from above', and both forcibly imposed their revolu-tionary ideology on other countries. Napoleon the pig is fierce-looking, 'not much of a talker, but with a reputation for getting his own way'. He dominates the party machinery, controls the educa-tion of the young and is superb at plotting and 'canvassing support for himself' between meetings.[15] Napoleon never presents any of his own plans and always criticizes Snowball's, though he eventually adopts these plans and even claims he invented them. He first distorts and then changes history, blames Snowball for all his own failures, accuses him of plotting with foreign enemies, drives him into exile and finally pronounces his death sentence. He also pub-lishes fantastic production figures, takes 'credit for every successful achievement and every stroke of good fortune', wins elections unanimously, names cities after himself and replaces the cult of Major ('the animals were required to file past the skull [Lenin's Tomb] in a reverent manner') with a more elaborate one of his own. As Orwell writes in 1941, 'One could not have a better example of the moral and emotional shallowness of our time, than the fact that we are now all more or less pro-Stalin. This disgusting murderer is temporarily on our side, and so the purges etc. are suddenly forgotten' (II.407).

The name Snowball recalls Trotsky's white hair and beard, and the fact that he melted before Stalin's opposition. Snowball is a brilliant speaker, sometimes unintelligible to the masses but always eloquent and impressive, more vivacious and inventive than Napoleon, and a much greater writer. He is also intellectual and energetic. For, as Deutscher writes of Trotsky in 1921, besides running the army and serving on the Politbureau,

> He was busy with a host of other assignments each of which would have made a full-time job for any man of less vitality and ability. He led, for instance, the Society of the Godless. . . . He was at this time Russia's chief intellectual inspirer and leading literary critic. He frequently addressed audiences.[16]

Orwell's description of Snowball's activities, though a comic parody, is close to reality:

> Snowball also busied himself with organising the other animals into what he called Animal Committees. . . . He formed the Egg Production Committee for the hens, the Clean Tails League for the cows, the Wild Comrades Re-education Committee . . . and various others, besides instituting classes in reading and writing.

Snowball studies military history, organizes, commands and leads the Army to victory in the Battle of the Cowshed (the Civil War) where foreign powers help Mr Jones and invade the farm (Russia). After the War he was 'full of plans for innovations and improvements'.

Two of the most important battles between Trotsky and Stalin are allegorized in the novel. Trotsky fought for the priority of manufacturing over agriculture and for accelerated industrialization,

and his ideas for the expansion of the Socialist sector of the economy
were eventually adopted by Stalin in the first five-year plan of 1928,
which called for collectivization of farms *and* for industrialization:
'Snowball conjured up pictures of fantastic machines which would
do their work for them while they grazed at their ease in the fields
... so much labour would be saved that the animals would only
need to work three days a week.' Stalin wanted comprehensive and
drastic collectivization: Napoleon 'argued that the great need of the
moment was to increase food production, and that if they wasted
time on the windmill they would all starve to death'.

In their central ideological conflict, Trotsky defended his idea of
'Permanent Revolution' against Stalin's theory of 'Socialism in One
Country'. Deutscher writes that 'Two rival and quasi-Messianic
beliefs seemed pitted against one another: Trotskyism with its faith
in the revolutionary vocation of the proletariat of the West; and
Stalinism with its glorification of Russia's socialist destiny.'[17]
Orwell presents this controversy in simpler but entirely accurate
words:

> According to Napoleon, what the animals must do was to procure fire-
> arms and train themselves in the use of them. According to Snowball,
> they must send out more and more pigeons and stir up rebellion among
> the animals on the other farms. The one argued that if they could not
> defend themselves they were bound to be conquered, the other argued
> that if rebellions happened everywhere they would have no need to
> defend themselves.

When Snowball comes to the crucial points in his speeches, 'It was
noticed that [the sheep] were especially liable to break into "Four
legs good, two legs bad",' just as in the party Congress in 1927,
at Stalin's instigation, 'pleas for the opposition were drowned in the
continual, hysterically intolerant uproar from the floor'.[18] The
Trotsky–Stalin conflict reached a crucial point in mid-1927, after
Britain broke diplomatic relations with Russia and ruined Stalin's
hopes for an agreement between Soviet and British trade unions;
the Russian ambassador to Poland was assassinated; and Chiang
Kai-shek massacred the Chinese Communists who had joined him

at Stalin's orders. Trotsky and the Opposition issued a declaration attacking Stalin for these political and military failures, but before they could bring this issue before the party Congress and remove, Stalin from power, he expelled Trotsky and Zinoviev from the Party.[19] Orwell writes of this vital moment in Soviet history, which signalled the final defeat of Trotsky, 'By the time he [Snowball] had finished speaking, there was no doubt as to the way the vote would go. But just at this moment' Napoleon's dogs (the GPU, or Secret Police) attacked Snowball and forced him to flee the farm and go into exile.

Orwell is not primarily interested in the practical or ideological merits of these controversies, for he believed (wrongly, I think) that *both* men had betrayed the revolution. He told a friend that 'Trotsky–Snowball was potentially as big a villain as Stalin–Napoleon, although he was Napoleon's victim. The first note of corruption was struck when the pigs secretly had the cows' milk added to their own mash and Snowball consented to this first act of inequity.'[20] And he writes in 1939, the year before Trotsky's murder, 'It is probably a good thing for Lenin's reputation that he died so early. Trotsky, in exile, denounces the Russian dictatorship, but he is probably as much responsible for it as any man now living, and there is no certainty that as a dictator he would be preferable to Stalin, though undoubtedly he has a much more interesting mind' (1.381).

The three main Russian political events that are most extensively allegorized in *Animal Farm* are the disastrous results of Stalin's forced collectivization (1929–33), the Great Purge Trials (1936–38) and the diplomacy with Germany that terminated with Hitler's invasion in 1941. Orwell writes that 'after Snowball's expulsion, the animals were somewhat surprised to hear Napoleon announce that the windmill was to be built after all'. The first demolition of the windmill, which Napoleon blames on Snowball, is the failure of the first five-year plan. The destructive methods of the hens during the 'Kronstadt Rebellion' – they 'made a determined effort to thwart Napoleon's wishes. Their method was to fly up to the rafters and there lay their eggs, which smashed to pieces on the floor' – are precisely those used by the *muzhiks* in 1929 to protest against the forced collectivization of their farms: 'In desperation they slaughtered their cattle, smashed implements, and burned crops. This was the *muzhiks*' great Luddite-like rebellion.'[21] The result of this enormous ruin was, as Orwell writes in a 1938 review of Lyons's book on Russia, 'years of appalling hardship, culminating in the Ukraine famine of 1933, in which a number estimated at not less than three million people starved to death' (1.334). Deutscher mentions the recurrent cannibalism during times of starvation,[22] and Orwell refers to this famine when he writes, 'It was being put about that all the animals were dying of famine and disease . . . and had resorted to cannibalism and infanticide.'

The most dramatic and emotional political events of the thirties were the Great Purge Trials, the minute details of which were published in the official translation of 1938. Stalin's motive, according to the editors of the trial's transcript, was a craving 'to achieve an unrestricted personal dictatorship with a totality of power that he did not yet possess in 1934'.[23] They also state that in the trial 'pieces of falsified real history have been woven along with outright fiction'.[24] A perfect example of this occurs when the animals 'remembered that at the critical moment of the battle Snowball had turned to flee', but forgot that it was a deliberate ruse to prepare the victorious ambush.

In the trial of Trotsky's friend Karl Radek, in February 1937, the prosecution claimed that Trotsky

> was organizing and directing industrial sabotage in the Soviet Union, catastrophes in coal mines, factories, and on the railways, mass poisonings of Soviet workers, and repeated attempts on the lives of Stalin and other members of the Politbureau.[25]

After the destruction of the windmill, Napoleon roars:

> thinking to set back our plans . . . this traitor has crept here under cover of night and destroyed our work of nearly a year. . . .
> A rumour went round that Snowball had after all contrived to introduce poison into Napoleon's food.

In the last and most important trial, that of Bukharin in March 1938, Gorky's secretary Kryuchkov confessed, 'I arranged long walks for Alexei Maximovich, I was always arranging bonfires. The smoke of the bonfire naturally affected Gorky's weak lungs.'[26] During the purge in *Animal Farm*, 'Two other sheep confessed to having murdered an old ram, an especially devoted follower of Napoleon, by chasing him round and round a bonfire when he was suffering from a cough.'[27]

In his review of Lyons's book, Orwell is horrified by the 'monstrous state trials at which people who have been in prison for months or years are suddenly dragged forth to make incredible confessions' (1.334); and, in his satire, 'A sheep confessed to having urinated in the drinking pool – urged to do this, so she said, by Snowball.' Tucker and Cohen state that nine million people were arrested during the purges, and that the number of people executed has been reliably estimated at three million.[28] In *Animal Farm*, all the 'guilty' animals are 'slain on the spot', and in a terrifying moment of the book, after the confessions and executions, 'there was a pile of corpses lying before Napoleon's feet and the air was heavy with the smell of blood'.

After solidifying his domestic power through massive liquidation, Stalin turned his attention to the increasing menace in Europe and attempted to play off the democracies against Hitler. Deutscher describes how

> He still kept his front doors open for the British and the French and confined the contact with the Germans to the back stairs. . . . It is still impossible to say confidently to which part of the game Stalin then attached the greatest importance: to the plot acted on the stage or to the subtle counter-plot.[29]

Similarly, the animals were amazed when they discovered that, during Napoleon's apparent friendship with Pilkington, he 'had really been in secret agreement with Frederick'. But Napoleon is sadly deceived: Frederick's bank notes (the Hitler–Stalin non-aggression pact of August 1939) are forgeries, and he attacks Animal Farm without warning and destroys the windmill. Orwell's letter to his publisher in 1945 gives a fascinating insight into the precision of his allegorical technique:

> When the windmill is blown up, I wrote 'all the animals including Napoleon flung themselves on their faces.' I would like to alter it to 'all the animals except Napoleon'. If the book has been printed it's not worth bothering about, but I just thought the alteration would be fair to Joseph Stalin, as he did stay in Moscow during the German advance (III.359).

Hitler's defeat in the Battle of Stalingrad (January 1943) was the turning point of the Russian campaign: when the enemy 'saw that they were in danger of being surrounded, Frederick shouted to his men to get out while the going was good, and the next moment the cowardly enemy was running for dear life'.

One of Stalin's diplomatic blunders is also portrayed by Orwell. The reappearance of the raven Moses 'after an absence of several years' and his eternal talk about the Sugarcandy Mountain represents Stalin's queer attempt, in the spring of 1944, at reconciliation with the Pope. In order to gain Catholic support for his Polish policy, he received a lowly and unaccredited American priest, Father Orlemanski, and 'was twice closeted with him for long hours' during a most crucial period of the war. Nothing came of this, of course, and the result of this stunt, writes Deutscher, was that Stalin was made 'the laughing-stock of the world'.[30]

The satire concludes, as Orwell says in the Preface, with the 1943 'Teheran Conference, which was taking place while I was writing' (III.406). Deutscher, who knew him, relates that Orwell was 'unshakably convinced that Stalin, Churchill, and Roosevelt consciously plotted to divide the world, and to divide it for good, among themselves, and to subjugate it in common. . . . "*They* are all power-hungry," he used to repeat.'[31] The disagreement between the allies and the beginning of the cold war is symbolized when Napoleon and Pilkington, both suspicious, 'played an ace of spades simultaneously'.

The political allegory of *Animal Farm*, whether specific or general, detailed or allusive, is pervasive, thorough and accurate, and the brilliance of the book becomes much clearer when the satiric allegory is compared to the political actuality. Critics who write, 'it makes a delightful children's story'[32] and who emphasize that 'the gaiety in his nature had completely taken charge'[33] are dimly unaware of the allegory's sophisticated art. Orwell wrote to Middleton Murry the year he finished the work, 'I consider that willingness to criticise Russia and Stalin is *the* test of intellectual honesty' (III.203), and by his own or any standard it is an honest and even a courageous book.

Though subtle and compressed, *Animal Farm* shares the serious theme of *Nostromo*: that once in power, the revolutionary becomes as tyrannical as his oppressor. For Orwell writes of the post-revolutionary farm:

> In the old days there had often been scenes of bloodshed equally terrible, but it seemed to all of them that it was far worse now that it was happening among themselves.

And Dr Monygham similarly condemns the cruel and unprincipled capitalistic revolutionaries:

> They have their law, and their justice. But it is founded on expediency, and is inhuman; it is without rectitude, without the continuity and the force that can be found only in a moral principle. The time approaches when all that . . . [it] stands for shall weigh as heavily upon the people as the barbarism, cruelty, and misrule of a few years back.

And Emilia Gould replies with deep grief: 'There was something inherent in the necessities of successful action which carried with it the moral degradation of the idea.'[34] In his final work, *1984*, Orwell portrays one man's valiant but ineffectual stand against an omnipotent world of moral and ideological degradation.

8   The Genesis of *1984*

> Orwell loved the past, hated the present and
> dreaded the future.
>
> MALCOLM MUGGERIDGE

THE MOST COMMON CLICHÉ of Orwell criticism is that *1984*
(1949) is a 'nightmare vision' of the future.[1] I believe, on the contrary, that it is a very concrete and naturalistic portrayal of the
present and the past, and that its great originality results more from
a realistic synthesis and rearrangement of familiar materials than
from any prophetic or imaginary speculations. *1984* is not only
a paradigm of the history of Europe for the previous twenty years,
but also a culmination of all the characteristic beliefs and ideas
expressed in Orwell's works from the Depression to the cold war.
The origins of the novel can be found in Orwell's earliest books,
and its major themes, precise symbols and specific passages can be
traced very exactly throughout his writings. For example, Orwell
characteristically expresses the poverty and isolation that oppresses
the characters in his novels in terms of personal humiliation, so that
Winston's sexual experience with his wife Katharine (who is frigid
like Elizabeth in *Burmese Days* and Dorothy in *A Clergyman's
Daughter*) is exactly like that of Gordon with Rosemary in *Keep the
Aspidistra Flying*.

Orwell felt he had to frighten people into a painful recognition
of the dangers that threatened their very existence. His statements
about *1984* reveal that the novel, though set in a future time, is
realistic rather than fantastic, and deliberately intensifies the actuality

of the present. Orwell writes that *1984* 'is a novel about the future
– that is, it is in a sense a fantasy, but in the form of a naturalistic
novel. . . . [It is] intended as a show-up of the perversions to which a
centralised economy is liable, and which have already been partly
realised in Communism and fascism. . . . Totalitarian ideas have
taken root in the minds of intellectuals everywhere, and I have tried
to draw these ideas out to their logical consequences' (IV.329–30,
502). Irving Howe (and the 'nightmare' critics who follow him)
asserts, 'It is extremely important to note that the world of *1984* is
not totalitarianism as we know it, but totalitarianism after its world
triumph.'[2] It would be more accurate to say that *1984* portrays the
very real though unfamiliar political terrorism of Nazi Germany
and Stalinist Russia transposed into the landscape of London in
1941–44.[3]

The naturalistic setting of wartime London is combined with brutal
characteristics of eighteenth-century England to emphasize the
moral and material regression under 'Ingsoc'. The people mollify
their miserable existence with large doses of acidic gin, prisoners
march through the streets in leg-irons and public hangings provide
popular amusement.[4] The major Augustan influence on *1984* is
Gulliver's Travels, especially Book III which, Orwell says, is an
attack on totalitarianism and 'an extraordinarily clear prevision of
the spy-haunted "police-State", with its endless heresy-hunts and
treason trials' (IV.213). Julia's mechanical job on the novel-writing
machines is clearly derived from the Engine in the Academy of
Lagado, 'so contrived, that the Words shifted into new Places, as
the square bits of Wood moved upside down'.[5] The absurd scientific
experiments described in Goldstein's book are very like those Swift
used to mock the Royal Society; and the 'Floating Fortress' is
reminiscent of Swift's 'Floating Island' that also reduces rebellious
subjects to obedience. In *1984* 'Newspeak was designed not to
extend but to *diminish* the range of thought, and this purpose was
indirectly assisted by cutting the choice of words down to a
minimum'; the Houyhnhnms have no word in their language to
express lying, falsehood or anything evil. And State control of love,

sex and marriage is similar in Houyhnhnmland and Oceania. Love is deliberately excluded from marriage, which is an objective and dispassionate conjunction for the sole purpose of propagation. It is arranged by the State or parents on a pragmatic basis, and adultery and fornication are forbidden or unknown.

Though Trafalgar is renamed Victory Square and Big Brother takes Nelson's place atop his column, the physical setting of Airstrip One is essentially that of Orwell's 'London Letters' to the *Partisan Review* (1941–46), just as the Ministry of Truth is based on his experience at the bureaucratic BBC. There is a continuous war, with air raids and underground shelters, rubble in the streets, a sense of disintegration and decay. There is rationing, a black market, *ersatz* sugar and coffee, and a constant shortage of small but essential articles like razor blades and boot polish.

The weapons and inventions of Oceania, which shows no material progress since 1949, are familiar and conventional: truncheons, machine-guns, grenades, bombs, rockets; and microphones, dictaphones ('speak-write'), two-way television ('telescreen'). When Orwell tries to be more sophisticated and imaginative about such things, he is rather unconvincing, as when Police Patrols snoop into windows with helicopters, and concealed microphones in the vast countryside not only pick up but also *recognize* voices.

'Orwell fascinates [East Europeans] through his insight into details they know well,' writes Czeslaw Milosz; 'they are amazed that a writer who never lived in Russia should have so keen a perception into its life.'[6] Orwell's acute understanding of totalitarianism is most strongly influenced by Trotsky's *The Revolution Betrayed* (1937), a passionate condemnation of the Stalin régime and the model for Goldstein's book. During the Moscow Purge Trials, Trotsky quoted Rakovsky (former Commissar and Ambassador who became an early victim of the purges) as saying:

> By means of demoralizing methods, which convert thinking Communists into machines, destroying will, character and human dignity, the ruling circles have succeeded in converting themselves into an unremovable and inviolate oligarchy, which replaces the class and the party.

And Trotsky's account of the secret police was noted by Orwell in his portrayal of child informers and the sudden 'vaporization' of those who, like Winston, are suspected of 'thoughtcrime':[7]

> The GPU introduces the sickening corruption of treachery and tale-bearing into the so-called 'socialist schools'. . . . All who are outstanding and unsubmissive in the ranks of the young are systematically destroyed, suppressed or physically exterminated.[8]

The illegal dated photograph of Jones, Aaronson and Rutherford that Winston finds is related to Trotsky and based on historical fact. All three men confessed that they had betrayed important military secrets to the enemy, and the photograph proved that 'the confessions were lies'. And Isaac Deutscher writes of the purge trials:

> In those few cases where the defendants did refer to specific circumstances . . . that could be verified, the falsehood of their confessions was immediately plain. A hotel in Copenhagen where three defendants, Holtzman, David and Berman-Yurin, had allegedly had an appointment with Trotsky, had ceased to exist many years before.[9]

In *1984*, the enormous face on the posters, 'with a heavy black moustache and ruggedly handsome features' and the caption 'BIG BROTHER IS WATCHING YOU', is based mainly on Stalin, but it also suggests the famous recruiting poster of 1914 with the picture of Field-Marshal Kitchener and the caption 'Your Country Needs YOU'. As in contemporary Russia, the people are called Comrade, the three-year plans are exceeded as the staggering figures of production output are announced, and women wear overalls and produce children for the State who are trained as informers and cause the extermination of their parents. The atmosphere of overpowering fear is reinforced by the well-known characteristics of the Nazi régime: the underground resistance cells, hysterial Nuremberg-like demonstrations, sadistic attacks on Goldstein and other Jews, and 'Facecrime', or having pronounced Semitic features.

History is completely rewritten, often in imitation of Stalin's military and pedantic style and his trick of answering his own rhetorical questions (Orwell also parodies Trotsky's style in Goldstein's book). It is not clear, however, *whom* the Party is trying to convince by its enormous historical revisions. Since it controls all books and media, it would seem more effective to destroy the old books and write new ones. Winston's contention that the publication of the suppressed photo would be enough to blow the Party to atoms seems highly unlikely.

The powerful sense of impending and then actual disaster that dominated Orwell's life and mind in the thirties and forties is, quite naturally, expressed in the books he wrote during the last twenty years of his life. As early as *Down and Out*, Orwell foresees 'some dismal Marxian Utopia' as the only alternative to the present conditions;[10] and three years later Gordon Comstock gloomily imagines a socialist future as 'some kind of Aldous Huxley *Brave New World*, only not so amusing'.[11] The following year, in *Wigan Pier*, Orwell states that 'for the vision of the totalitarian state there is being substituted the vision of the totalitarian world', and that 'we are living in a world in which nobody is free, in which hardly anybody is secure, in which it is almost impossible to be honest and remain alive'.[12] And, in *Coming Up For Air*, George Bowling accurately prophesies not only the imminent war but also the world of 1984 that Orwell writes about ten years later:

> The coloured shirts, the barbed wire, the rubber truncheons. The secret cells where the electric light burns night and day, and the detectives watching you while you sleep. And the processions and the posters with enormous faces, and the crowds of a million people all cheering for the leader till they deafen themselves into thinking that they really worship him. . . . It's all going to happen.[13]

And there is a direct line of political thought from *Homage to Catalonia* through *Animal Farm* to *1984*, all three of which could be called 'The Revolution Betrayed'. Orwell's last novel had been germinating in his mind for a very long time.

The genesis of *1984* becomes even clearer when the evolution of three symbolic images is traced. The most famous and frequently quoted symbol is O'Brien's picture of the future: 'Imagine a boot stamping on a human face – forever.' Orwell had read a variation of this phrase in Book IV of *Gulliver's Travels* when Gulliver imagines the Houyhnhnms 'battering the Warriors' Faces into Mummy, by terrible Yerks from their hinder Hoofs'.[14] This image also appears in another source of *1984*, Jack London's *The Iron Heel*, when the upright hero, Ernest Everhard, predicts that 'the Iron Heel will walk upon our faces'.[15] In *Coming Up For Air*, Bowling varies this image slightly in his vision 'of himself smashing people's faces in with a spanner';[16] and in *The Lion and the Unicorn* (1941), Orwell makes the specific connection between totalitarianism and this inhuman cruelty when he writes that the Nazi goose-step 'is simply an affirmation of naked power; contained in it, quite consciously and intentionally, is the vision of a boot crashing down on a face' (II.62). In a weary letter of 1943, he calls himself 'an orange that's been trodden on by a very dirty boot' (II.304). The next year, Orwell says that 'Giants stamping on pygmies is the characteristic pattern of our age';[17] and in 'Raffles and Miss Blandish' he quotes, with revulsion, Chase's description of 'stamping on somebody's face and then, having crushed the man's mouth in, grinding his heel round and round in it' (III.218). This image of merciless sadism is one that Orwell could never exorcise from his mind, for it symbolized the connection between brutality, power worship, nationalism and totalitarianism.

Another horrible and unforgettable symbol is rats. Their ugliness and ferocity cause nightmares, panic and convulsions of nausea in Winston, and they are later used by O'Brien to torture and destroy him. In Book II of *Gulliver's Travels*, Gulliver is assaulted by two rats who 'came up almost to my Face; whereupon I rose in a Fright. . . . These horrible Animals had the Boldness to attack me on both Sides.'[18] Another possible influence is Camus' *The Plague* (1947), an allegory of the Nazi occupation of France, whose theme is analogous to *1984* and those central metaphor is a disease caused by rats. The rat image appears in almost every one of Orwell's works. In *Down and Out* a Parisian brothel smells of rats; in *Burmese Days* the treacherous U Po Kyin fears he will be reincarnated as a rat; and in *Keep the Aspidistra Flying* Comstock's landlady speaks of young women as if they were 'plague-rats'. In *Wigan Pier*, the rat image takes on the disturbing psychological connotations of *1984*: 'Going into the dark doorway of that common lodging-house seemed to me like going down into some dreadful subterranean place – a sewer full of rats, for instance.'[19] In *Homage to Catalonia*, rats run over Orwell in the darkness; and in *Coming Up For Air* he repeats an image from *Homage*, when Bowling shelters himself from a bomb and is 'flattened out on the pavement like a rat when it squeezes under a door'.[20] In *Animal Farm*, 'while Major was speaking four large rats had crept out of their holes', and when these rats become troublesome, they are said to be 'in league with Snowball'.[21] In *1984*, the battered slum doorways 'were somehow curiously suggestive of rat holes', and they continue to appear as a disturbing *leitmotif* throughout the novel. Rats invade the secret room where Winston and Julia meet, and are associated in Winston's mind with something dreadful and unendurable on the other side of a 'wall of darkness'. This wall of darkness is also related to the secure 'place where there is no darkness', where Winston hopes to meet O'Brien. Ultimately, this place becomes the constantly-lighted Ministry of Love where O'Brien uses rats to break Winston's will and force him to betray Julia.

The most convincing evidence for the evolution from Orwell's earlier works of the characteristic beliefs and ideas of *1984* is the specific passages that are repeated almost exactly in the last book. There are two principal reasons for this. First, as John Wain notes, Orwell 'was a man of comparatively few ideas, which he took every opportunity of putting across';[22] and second, Orwell was so seriously ill that he feared he might die before finishing the novel. After the book was published, he told Julian Symons: 'You are of course right abt the vulgarity of the "Room 101" business. I was aware of this while writing it, but I didn't know another way of getting somewhere near the effect I wanted' (IV.502–3). Orwell wrote the novel as quickly and easily as possible, drawing freely from his previous books when they could serve his purpose, and he succeeded despite severe limitations.

The tenements and slums of the proles, and the warmth and vitality that flourish amid this economic deprivation, derive from Orwell's experiences in Paris and Wigan as well as from his portrayal of wartime London. For the working-class district of Paris where Orwell lived in 1928–29 is reproduced almost exactly in the opening pages of *1984*; and the nineteenth-century slums of the industrial Midlands are still standing in Oceania: 'The houses are poky and ugly, and insanitary and comfortless, and they are distributed in incredibly filthy slums.'[23] The simple comforts of working-class life – 'Your pipe drawing sweetly, the sofa cushions are soft underneath you, the fire is well alight, the air warm and stagnant' (IV.98) – are also praised in *1984*, when Winston enjoys the privacy of the old armchair and fireplace in Charrington's room above the antique shop that he associates with ancestral memories of 'pre-revolutionary times'. And these somnolent and ignorant proles represent the same revolutionary hope as the exploited beasts of *Animal Farm*: 'But the proles, if only they could somehow become conscious of their own strength, would have no need to conspire. They needed only to rise up and shake themselves like a horse.'

The absolute control of individual thought and action by the State is another theme that dominates Orwell's works. An idea that he frequently repeats and adopts for *1984* is that 'In the end the Party would announce that two and two made five, and you would have to believe it.' This idea appears as early as 1939 in his review of Bertrand Russell's book on power:

> It is quite possible that we are descending into an age in which two and two will make five when the Leader says so. Mr Russell points out that the huge system of organised lying upon which the dictators depend keeps their followers out of contact with reality. (I.376)

In Orwell's novel, the régime is so repressive that it is able to disintegrate totally the personality of those who resist and to make the Winston Smiths believe what they know to be false.

Orwell's belief that 'history has stopped' and is being re-written first appears in 1943, and is reaffirmed by Winston. ' "History stopped in 1936". . . . If the leader says of such and such an event, "It never happened" – well, it never happened. . . . This prospect frightens me much more than bombs' (II.256,259). For Winston, the psychological effect of political oppression is the loss of childhood memories, the abolition of history in microcosm. In 1939, Orwell is concerned about the extreme changes in history and traditions and asks, 'Is life – life for the ordinary person – any better in Russia than it was before?' (I.379); and he repeats this question in his last two books, when the older animals rack their dim memories and try to decide whether things had been worse under Mr Jones, and when Winston asks the proles about life in the days before the Revolution.

The central concept in the ideology of the Party, that freedom and happiness cannot coexist, evolves from Dostoyevsky's *The Brothers Karamazov* by way of Zamyatin's *We*. In Dostoyevsky, the totalitarian Grand Inquisitor questions the ordinary man's capacity for freedom and ironically

> claims it as a great merit for himself and his Church that at last they have vanquished freedom and have done so to make men happy.[24]

In his review of Zamyatin's novel, Orwell states that

> The guiding principle of his State is that happiness and freedom are incompatible. . . . The Single State has restored happiness by removing this freedom. (IV.73)

And O'Brien, the modern Grand Inquisitor in *1984*, informs Winston that

> the choice for mankind lay between freedom and happiness, and for the great bulk of mankind, happiness was better.

The horrible irony, of course, is that the people of *1984* have neither freedom nor happiness. The omnipotence of the Church and State is defended by the Grand Inquisitor (and by O'Brien) who maintains that men are terribly weak and unable to choose between good and evil. He tells Christ that 'man is weaker and baser by nature than Thou hast believed him! . . . By showing him so much respect, Thou didst, as it were, cease to feel for him, for Thou didst ask too much from him.'[25]

A description of the genesis of *1984* reveals the remarkable consistency of Orwell's style and long-considered ideas, and the workings of his creative imagination, which drew upon his experiences of poverty and totalitarianism; his reading of Swift, Dostoyevsky, Zamyatin and Trotsky; and the recurring motifs of his earlier works. The least effective parts of the novel are the purely expository passages where he establishes the future state of the world in *1984*: the political events that followed the Atomic War (as revealed in Goldstein's book), Winston's 'historical' work at the Ministry of Truth, and the Appendix on Newspeak.

The most powerful and effective part of *1984* is Orwell's recreation of the ghastly atmosphere of fear and torture in the extermination camps. Bruno Bettelheim writes that one major goal of the Gestapo was 'to break the prisoners as individuals, and to change them into a docile mass from which no individual or group act of resistance could arise. . . . [The concentration camp] was a final apotheosis of the mass state, composed of a few depersonalized managers and millions of dehumanized slaves, all under thrall to one charismatic leader, the only "person", the only one truly alive.'[26] Like these prisoners, Winston must face the problem of individual existence in the literal, not the philosophical, sense. He does not attempt to define existence, but to discover *how* to exist. The paradox of totalitarianism is that it intensifies personal solitude when it forces all the isolated figures into one overpowering system.

The dominant emphasis throughout Orwell's work is on loneliness and exclusion, on the fearful individual in an oppressed world, on the people, in Trotsky's phrase, 'swept into the dustbin of history'. Winston Smith, the final embodiment of defeated man, has predecessors in all of Orwell's books: in his impoverished and exploited *personae* in Paris, London, Wigan and Spain; in Flory, Dorothy Hare, Gordon Comstock, George Bowling and Boxer. Each character attempts, in Chekhov's words, 'to squeeze the slave out of himself, drop by drop, and wake one beautiful morning to feel that he has no longer a slave's blood in his veins but a real man's'.[27] And each Orwell character struggles against the bondage of his threatening world toward individual freedom and responsibility.

Like the novels of Malraux and Sartre, *1984* expresses man's fears of isolation and disintegration, cruelty and dehumanization. Orwell's response to the horrors of contemporary history emphasizes his close relationship to these authors and firmly places him in the tradition described by Victor Brombert:

> Europe's dark hours are thus responsible for the emergence of a generation that feels '*située*' and responsible in the face of history – a generation whipped on by the urge to transmute its anguish into action. . . . Sartre has shown how the awareness of death, the threatened subjection to torture and the systematic will to degrade brought writers to the extreme frontiers of the human condition and inspired them with a . . . concern for moral issues.[28]

Orwell's repetition of obsessive ideas is an apocalyptic lamentation for the fate of modern man. His expression of the political experience of an entire generation gives *1984* a veritably mythic power and makes it one of the most influential books of the age, even for those who have never read it. As Harold Rosenberg states, 'The tone of the post-war imagination was set by Orwell's *1984*: since the appearance of that work, [the theme of] the "dehumanized collective" haunts our thoughts.'[29] Orwell's unique contribution to English literature is a passionate commitment, a radical sincerity and an ethic of responsibility that ultimately transcends his defeated heroes.

Conclusion: Critics on Orwell

APART FROM NUMEROUS book reviews, there was little written about Orwell during his lifetime. Cyril Connolly's *Enemies of Promise*, which was published in 1938 when Orwell was not very well known, described him as a boy at St Cyprian's and Eton; and it provided an interesting contrast to Orwell's own bitter memories when 'Such, Such Were the Joys' appeared posthumously in 1952. Orwell's friend, George Woodcock, published the first serious essays about him in 1946 and 1948, before the publication of *1984*, and made a fundamental criticism of Orwell's two weaknesses: 'the failure to penetrate deeply into the rooted causes of injustices and lies against which he fights, and the lack of any real constructive vision for the future of man'.[1] Victor Pritchett contributed a brief appreciation of Orwell in *Living Writers* (1947); and in his important obituary of 1950, he called him 'a kind of saint'.[2] Arthur Koestler's obituary also emphasized his moral example and said that he was 'the only writer of genius among the *littérateurs* of social revolt between the two wars'.[3] Since then Orwell the man has attracted nearly as much admiration as Orwell the writer.

After Orwell's death his major essays were collected and published as *Shooting an Elephant* (1950), *Such, Such Were the Joys* (1953), *England Your England* (1953); and his *Collected Essays, Journalism and Letters* (1968) have appeared in four volumes. His works have been published in both standard and paperback editions in England and America, and he has been translated into more than sixty languages.

Most of the seventeen studies on Orwell are competent. Tom

Hopkinson's British Council pamphlet appeared in 1953. The first
two books on Orwell were published in 1954 by John Atkins and
Laurence Brander, who had known him in the forties and who
provided basic surveys of his work. Two years later Christopher
Hollis, who was Orwell's contemporary at Eton and had met him
briefly in Burma, added some biographical information but wrote
the same sort of book. In 1961 Orwell's closest friend, Sir Richard
Rees, published his book, subtitled 'Fugitive From the Camp of
Victory'; and though this contributed some useful ideas about
Orwell, it was disappointing as criticism.

In 1961 the first scholarly book on Orwell by Richard Voorhees,
an American professor who did not know him personally and was
therefore more objective, analysed his paradoxical attitudes
about rebellion and responsibility, power and Socialism. Edward
Thomas wrote an introduction to Orwell for a series of books
on modern writers in 1965. The next year George Woodcock
published the best book on Orwell, *The Crystal Spirit*, which
provided the fullest biographical discussion of the man, and the
most careful explication of his fiction, his political ideas and his
criticism. B. T. Oxley published another introductory book in
1967; and in 1968 Jenni Calder's comparison of Orwell and Koestler
as revolutionaries and prophets provided many valuable insights
about their social and political thought. In contrast to this, Ruth
Ann Lief's book seemed weak and unsatisfactory. Two more
scholarly books, by Robert Lee and Keith Alldritt, appeared in
1969. The former was devoted to Orwell's fiction, and the latter
was especially good on his development as a writer.

The four books on Orwell published during 1971-72 deserve a
somewhat fuller discussion. *The World of George Orwell*, a collection
of essays with photographs edited by Miriam Gross, attempts to see
him 'both in terms of what he means today and as a man whose
achievement very much needs to be set in the context of his own
period'.[4] Though the book contains perceptive essays by William
Empson and Malcolm Muggeridge, who knew Orwell, most of the
contributions are too short for an extended argument, and lack

originality and intellectual substance. Raymond Williams's book in the Fontana Modern Masters series is a Marxist attack on Orwell as a reactionary and a revisionist who made an unacceptable accommodation to capitalism. It recalls the extreme Left-wing condemnation of Orwell's books from *The Road to Wigan Pier* to *1984*.

David Kubal's *Outside the Whale* is a rather superficial attempt to connect the two main divisions, literary and political, in Orwell's work. Peter Stansky and William Abrahams's *The Unknown Orwell* is a biography of his first thirty years, and culminates in the publication of *Down and Out in Paris and London*. Though it brings together much useful information about Orwell, it does not fulfil the claim of its title. The authors present a familiar figure, and merely fill in the details of a picture that remains substantially the same. The theme of the book, that 'Blair was the man to whom things happened; Orwell the man who wrote about them,'[5] is hardly convincing because they do not show that Orwell changed his personality when he changed his name. He had the same characteristic strength and integrity before 1933 as he did after he published his first book.

The articles on Orwell fall into two categories: biographical and critical. Beadon, Dunn, Fen, Heppenstall, Morris, Potts, Powell, Symons and Warburg have written interesting anecdotal reminiscences; and all but those of Morris and Heppenstall (the latter got drunk and was beaten up by Orwell when they shared a London flat in 1935) were extremely favourable. Powell was the most perceptive about his paradoxical and individualistic character, and Warburg was excellent on the publishing background of *Animal Farm* and *1984*.

Scholars have written on Orwell in Serbo-Croat, Dutch, Norwegian, Finnish, Hungarian and Japanese as well as in French, Italian and German. There have been critical essays on his attitude toward imperialism, Socialism and Communism; on his relation to Dickens, Gissing and Kipling; on his criticism, style, patriotism and nostalgia for the past. Two poems have been written about Orwell; several very thorough bibliographies of his extensive uncollected writings have been compiled; and in 1950 a special issue of

World Review with contributions by Bertrand Russell, Stephen
Spender, Aldous Huxley, Herbert Read and Malcolm Muggeridge
was devoted to him.

E. M. Forster wrote in 1950 of Orwell's peculiar combination of
gaiety and grimness, and said that 'He found much to discomfort
him in his world and desired to transmit it, and in *1984* he extended
discomfort into agony. . . . *1984* crowned his work, and it is under-
standably a crown of thorns.'[6] Lionel Trilling's 'George Orwell and
the Politics of Truth' (1952), which was written as the introduction
to the American paperback edition of *Homage to Catalonia*, was
probably the most influential essay on Orwell. Trilling believed that
'*Homage to Catalonia* is one of the most important documents of our
time. . . . It is a testimony to the nature of modern political life. It is
also a demonstration on the part of its author of one of the right
ways of confronting that life.'[7]

John Wain has written the best criticism of Orwell in the review
essays that have appeared in British magazines during the last
twenty years. In his *Spectator* review Wain emphasized the importance of Orwell's campaign for clearer thinking and writing; and in
'The Last of George Orwell' he argued that 'as a novelist Orwell was
not particularly gifted but as a controversial critic and pamphleteer
he was superb, as good as any in English literature'.[8] 'Orwell in
Perspective' discussed Orwell's effectiveness as a writer of polemic
and the relation of his style to his character, and 'Here Lies Lower
Binfield' suggested that the difference between Orwell and ordinary
Socialists was revealed in his ambivalent attitude toward the recent
past, which he expressed in *Coming Up For Air*.

Between 1966 and 1969 Muste, Benson, Weintraub and Hoskins
considered Orwell's contribution to the literature of the Spanish
Civil War. His essays on popular culture have influenced sociological
critics like Richard Hoggart, who has written a particularly good
essay on the contradictions in *The Road to Wigan Pier* 'between an
absolutist and a tolerantly resilient man, out to get things done by
communal political action, and a dark despairer; between the one
who urged the need for revolutionary changes in our thinking and a

man with a deep-seated sense that things would always go on much as they always had'.[9]

Most of the criticism has focused on Orwell's most famous and influential book, *1984*, which created the concepts of Doublethink, Newspeak and Big Brother. Bertrand Russell has remarked on Orwell's 'incapacity for comfortable illusion' and warned of the dangerous symptoms of *1984*; Stephen Spender has discussed the anti-Utopian aspects; Anthony West has examined the biographical implications; Isaac Deutscher, the biographer of Trotsky, has discussed Orwell's fear of the future and what he called 'the mysticism of cruelty'; and Irving Howe, in an important essay, introduced the 'nightmare' interpretation. Other scholars have compared Orwell to Zamyatin, Huxley, James Burnham and writers of science fiction; studied his irony, satire, parody, prophecy, psychology, masochism and theory of language.

Some important books on Orwell will soon be published. The special issue of *Modern Fiction Studies* in the spring of 1975, and the volume on him in the Twentieth Century Views series, will provide a fresh appraisal of his works. Alex Zwerdling's study of Orwell's politics, the second volume of Stansky and Abrahams's book, Bernard Crick's authorized biography and my anthology, *Orwell: The Critical Heritage,* should make important contributions to Orwell scholarship. Orwell's reputation has risen steadily since his death in 1950 and is now firmly established; and he is more widely read than perhaps any other serious writer of the twentieth century.

NOTES ON THE TEXT
BIBLIOGRAPHY
INDEX

NOTES ON THE TEXT

All references to books by George Orwell are to the Penguin editions; other references to his writings are to *The Collected Essays, Journalism and Letters of George Orwell*, eds. Sonia Orwell and Ian Angus (London, 1968).

Introduction

1 Samuel Johnson, *Rasselas* (1759), chapter 46.
2 E. M. Forster, 'George Orwell' in *Two Cheers For Democracy* (London, 1951), p. 72.
3 *The Collected Essays, Journalism and Letters of George Orwell*, eds. Sonia Orwell and Ian Angus, Vol. II (London, 1968), p. 15. Subsequent citations to volume and page refer to this edition.
4 *The Collected Letters of D. H. Lawrence*, ed. Harry Moore, Vol. I (New York, 1962), p. 204 (to A. W. McLeod, April 1913).
5 John Wain, 'Orwell in Perspective' in *New World Writing* XII (1957), 86.
6 *The Notebooks of Samuel Butler*, ed. Henry Jones (New York, 1917), p. 187.
7 *Ibid.*, p. 107. See also T. E. Lawrence's similar statement in *Men in Print* (London, 1940), p. 44: 'Prose is bad when people stop to look at it.'

1   The Autobiographical Strain

1 George Orwell, *The Road to Wigan Pier* (Harmondsworth, 1962), p. 106.
2 G. S. Fraser, *Lawrence Durrell: A Study* (London, 1968), p. 31.
3 William Thackeray, *The Newcomes* in *Works*, ed. George Saintsbury, Vol. XIV (London, 1908), p. 66.

4 Rudyard Kipling, 'Baa Baa Black Sheep' in *Works* (New York, n.d.), pp. 960, 975.

5 George Orwell, *Coming Up For Air* (Harmondsworth, 1962), p. 134.

6 See Gordon Ray, *Thackeray: The Uses of Adversity* (New York, 1955), p. 62: 'In later life Thackeray's recollections of his first years in his "native country" were scanty. He "could just remember" his father, writes Lady Ritchie, "a very tall, thin man, rising out of a bath".'

7 Quoted in Peter Stansky and William Abrahams, *The Unknown Orwell* (London, 1972), p. 125.

8 Quoted in *ibid.*, p. 73.

9 *The Road to Wigan Pier*, p. 104. See also *Coming Up For Air* (1939), p. 46; 'Boys' Weeklies' (1940), 1.473; 'Decline of the English Murder' (1946), IV.98; and *1984* (Harmondsworth, 1973), p. 80.

10 Hare, the name of the heroine in *A Clergyman's Daughter*, was the name of Orwell's paternal grandmother.

11 See *Letters of Sigmund Freud*, ed. Ernst Freud (London, 1961), p. 391: 'What makes all autobiographies worthless is, after all, their mendacity.'

12 Cyril Connolly, *Enemies of Promise* (London, 1938), pp. 211–13.

13 *Ibid.*, p. 213.

14 Quoted in Stansky and Abrahams, p. 52.

15 James Joyce, *A Portrait of the Artist as a Young Man* (New York, 1956), p. 50.

16 Quoted in G. K. Chesterton, *Charles Dickens* (New York, 1965), p. 37.

17 Rudyard Kipling, *Something of Myself* (New York, 1937), p. 17.

18 Charles Dickens, Preface to *Nicholas Nickleby* (London, 1964), p. xvi.

19 *Ibid.*, p. 87.

20 George Orwell, *A Clergyman's Daughter* (Harmondsworth, 1964), p. 187.

21 *Nicholas Nickleby*, p. 88.

22 *A Clergyman's Daughter*, p. 208.

23 Charles Dickens, *David Copperfield* (New York, 1950), p. 91.

24 *A Clergyman's Daughter*, p. 191.

25 *David Copperfield*, p. 92.

26 *Ibid.*, p. 91.

27 *A Clergyman's Daughter*, p. 218. See James Boswell, *Life of*

Johnson (London, 1961), p. 34: 'My master whipt me very well. Without that, Sir, I should have done nothing. . . . A child is afraid of being whipped and gets his task, and there's an end on't.'

28 *A Clergyman's Daughter*, p. 206.

29 George Orwell, *Keep the Aspidistra Flying* (Harmondsworth, 1962), p. 42.

30 *Ibid.*, p. 46.

31 *The Collected Letters of D. H. Lawrence*, ed. Harry Moore, Vol. I (New York, 1962), p. 234 (to A. W. McLeod, 26 October 1913).

32 Bruno Bettelheim, *The Informed Heart* (Glencoe, Illinois, 1960), pp. 129, 131, 230.

33 *Ibid.*, p. 297n.

34 Anthony West, 'George Orwell' in *Principles and Persuasions* (London, 1958), pp. 156, 158.

35 George Orwell, *1984* (Harmondsworth, 1973), p. 12.

36 Quoted in Sybille Bedford, *Aldous Huxley: A Biography*, Vol. I (London, 1973), p. 92.

37 *Keep the Aspidistra Flying*, p. 13.

38 Ray, p. 67.

39 Stansky and Abrahams, p. 149. Leonard Woolf's *Growing* (1961) and Philip Woodruff's *The Men Who Ruled India* (1954) describe the social and political background of Orwell's Burmese period.

40 Quoted in Stansky and Abrahams, p. 161.

41 Roger Beadon, 'With Orwell in Burma' in *Listener* LXXXI (29 May 1969), 755.

42 Joseph Conrad, 'Outpost of Progress' in *Tales of Heroes and History* (New York, 1960), p. 251.

43 Avril Dunn, 'My Brother, George Orwell' in *Twentieth Century* CLXIX (March 1961), 257.

44 Elisaveta Fen, 'George Orwell's First Wife' in *Twentieth Century* CLXVIII (August 1960), 115.

45 Anthony Powell, 'George Orwell: A Memoir' in *Atlantic Monthly* CCXX (October 1967), 65.

46 Fredric Warburg, *All Authors Are Equal* (London, 1973), p. 38.

47 George Woodcock, *The Crystal Spirit: A Study of George Orwell* (London, 1967), p. 11.

48 John Morris, '"Some Are More Equal Than Others": A Note on George Orwell' in *Penguin New Writing* XL (1950), 90.

49 Woodcock, p. 18.

50 T. S. Eliot, letter to George Orwell, 13 July 1944, in *The Times* (London) (6 January 1969), p. 9.

51 Dr Maurice Fishberg, *Pulmonary Tuberculosis*, quoted in Lewis Moorman, *Tuberculosis and Genius* (Chicago, 1940), p. xxix.

52 See Orwell's letter to his sister-in-law, Dr Gwen O'Shaughnessy, 1 January 1948, from a Glasgow hospital:

> They first crushed the phrenic nerve, which I gather is what makes the lung expand and contract, & then pumped air into the diaphragm, which I understand is to push the lung into a different position. (IV.391)

53 West, p. 158.

54 Lawrence and Orwell were treated by the same tuberculosis specialist, who in both cases was consulted too late. See George Zytaruk (ed.), 'The Last Days of D. H. Lawrence: Hitherto Unpublished Letters of Dr Andrew Morland' in *D. H. Lawrence Review* I (1968), 44–50.

2 The Essays

1 In 'Politics vs. Literature' Orwell writes that 'the inter-connection between Swift's [Tory] political loyalties and his ultimate despair is one of the most interesting features' of *Gulliver's Travels* (IV.207).

2 J.-K. Huysmans, *Against Nature* (Harmondsworth, 1959), p. 109.

3 The Ethics of Responsibility: *Burmese Days*

1 Stephen Spender, *World Within World* (Berkeley, 1966), p. 202.

2 Victor Brombert, *The Intellectual Hero* (Chicago, 1964), pp. 143, 147, 220, 218.

3 Orwell also wrote about imperialism in his essays 'Rudyard Kipling' and 'Reflections on Gandhi', and in the last half of *The Road to Wigan Pier*. His seven uncollected reviews and articles on Burma are the following:
'Note to *Whitehall's Road to Mandalay* by Robert Duval' in *Tribune* (London) 327 (2 April 1943), 12.
'Burma' in *Tribune* (London) 330 (23 April 1943), 13.
'War in Burma' in *New Statesman and Nation* XXVI (14 August 1943), 109–10.

'Behind the Ranges' in *Oberver* 7985 (11 June 1944), 3.

'Burma Roads' in *Observer* 8001 (1 October 1944), 3.

'Direct Rule May Return to Burma' in *New Vision* XIX (Autumn 1944), 6–9.

'Burmese Days' in *Observer* 8074 (24 February 1946), 3.

See also: I.306–7; III.210–12; III.355–7; IV.111–14, IV.281–2.

4 George Orwell, *The Road to Wigan Pier* (Harmondsworth, 1962), pp. 126, 129.

5 *Ibid.*, p. 130.

6 *Ibid.*, p. 97. In 'Why I Write', Orwell suggests the limitations of this novel: 'I wanted to write enormous naturalistic novels with unhappy endings, full of detailed descriptions and arresting similes, and also full of purple passages in which words were used partly for the sake of their sound. And in fact my first completed novel, *Burmese Days*, which I wrote when I was thirty but projected much earlier, is rather that kind of book' (I.3).

7 Compare Joseph Conrad, *Lord Jim* (New York, 1931), p. 259, with *Burmese Days* (Harmondsworth, 1967), pp. 5, 14:

Doramin was one of the most remarkable men of his race I have ever seen. His bulk for a Malay was immense, but he did not look merely fat; he looked imposing, monumental. This motionless body [was] clad in rich stuffs, coloured silks, gold embroideries ... the flat, big, round face [was] wrinkled, furrowed. ... When he walked, two short, sturdy young fellows ... sustained his elbows; they would ease him down and stand behind his chair till he wanted to rise ... and then they would catch him under his armpits and help him up. ... It was generally believed he consulted his wife as to public affairs.

Unblinking, rather like a great porcelain idol, U Po Kyin gazed out into the fierce sunlight. He was a man of fifty, so fat that for years he had not risen from his chair without help. ... His face was vast, yellow and quite unwrinkled. ... He wore one of those vivid Arakenese *longyis* with green and magenta checks. ... [His wife] had been the confidente of U Po Kyin's intrigues for twenty years and more.

8 In a kind of adolescent joke, Orwell names this aristocratic but nasty character, who is similar to the snobs at school, after Dr A. W. Verrall, the industrious editor of Greek and Latin textbooks.

9 For a thorough discussion of this question, see my book *Fiction*

and the Colonial Experience (Ipswich, Suffolk and Totowa, N.J., 1973).

10 Friedrich Nietzsche, 'Notes' (1874) in *The Portable Nietzsche*, ed. Walter Kaufmann (New York, 1954), p. 48.

11 D. H. Lawrence's story 'Fanny and Annie' (1921), in which a young man is publicly denounced by the mother of his pregnant mistress while in church with his fiancée, probably suggested this incident to Orwell.

12 Lionel Trilling, 'George Orwell and the Politics of Truth' in *The Opposing Self* (London, 1955), p. 161.

13 *The Short Stories of Ernest Hemingway* (New York, 1938), p. 15.

4   The Honorary Proletarian: Orwell and Poverty

1 George Orwell, *Down and Out in Paris and London* (Harmondsworth, 1940), p. 130.

2 George Orwell, *Burmese Days* (Harmondsworth, 1967), p. 66.

3 *Down and Out*, p. 104.

4 George Orwell, 'Culture and Democracy' in *Victory or Vested Interests?* ed. G. D. H. Cole (London, 1942), p. 81.

5 G. B. Shaw, Preface to *Immaturity* in *Selected Prose* (New York, 1952), p. 54.

6 'Culture and Democracy', p. 83.

7 See Henry Mayhew, 'Of the Filth, Dishonesty, and Immorality of Low Lodging Houses' in *London Labour and the London Poor* (London, 1965), p. 54:

> A person, once well off, who has sunk into the very depths of poverty, often makes his first appearance in one of the worst of those places. Perhaps it is because he keeps away from them as long as he can, and then, in a sort of desperation fit, goes into the cheapest he meets with; or if he knows it's a vile place, he very likely says to himself, I may as well know the worst at once. . . . When a man's lost caste in society, he may as well go the whole hog, bristles and all, and a low lodging-house is the entire pig.

8 Jack London, *The People of the Abyss* (New York, 1903), p. 1.

9 *Down and Out*, p. 150.

10 George Orwell, Introduction to *British Pamphleteers* (London, 1948), p. 9.

11 A passage from 'The Life of a Flower Girl' in Henry Mayhew's

London Labour and the London Poor, p. 65, is very similar to Dorothy's experience as a hop-picker:

She then went into Kent, hop-picking, and there fell in with a beggar, who accosted her while she was sitting under a tree. He said, 'You have got a very bad pair of shoes on; come with me, and you shall have some better ones.' She consented, and walked with him into the village close by.

12 The opening paragraphs of chapter one, part three, are a good example of Orwell's 'lifeless' style. See *A Clergyman's Daughter* (Harmondsworth, 1964), pp. 30–1.

13 Orwell may have taken Warburton's name from the English lord who unsuccessfully proposes to Isabel Archer in James's *The Portrait of a Lady* (1881).

14 Orwell was probably influenced by Lawrence's Alvina Houghton, the *déclassé* heroine in *The Lost Girl* (1921).

15 George Woodcock, *The Crystal Spirit: A Study of George Orwell* (Boston, 1966), p. 133.

16 *A Clergyman's Daughter*, p. 220.

17 George Orwell, *Coming Up For Air* (Harmondsworth, 1962), p. 31.

18 E. M. Forster, 'What I Believe' in *Two Cheers For Democracy* (London, 1951), p. 77.

19 Ravelston is based on Orwell's friend Sir Richard Rees who was the editor of *Adelphi* where Orwell published the mediocre poem that Gordon composes in the novel. Rosemary is based on his wife, Eileen.

20 George Orwell, *Keep the Aspidistra Flying* (Harmondsworth, 1962), pp. 11–12.

21 *Down and Out*, p. 176.

22 The influence of *Keep the Aspidistra Flying* on Wain's *Hurry on Down* (Harmondsworth, 1960) is particularly strong, as the following Orwellian quotations from Wain indicate:

His aim was to be outside the class structure altogether (52).

He began to think increasingly about money. The poison was doing its work (77).

He had turned his back resolutely on the world represented by Robert Tharkles; he had declared that he wanted none of it, that he would manage without its aid or approval (81).

Can't get a short drink under two bob. Money. The network everywhere: no, a web, sticky and cunningly arranged (84).

23 Letter from George Gissing to Morley Roberts, February 1895,
   quoted in Jacob Korg, 'The Spiritual Theme in George
   Gissing's *Born in Exile*' in *From Jane Austen to Joseph Conrad*,
   eds. Robert Rathburn and Martin Steinmann, Jr (Minneapolis,
   1958), p. 246.
24 George Gissing, *New Grub Street* (Boston, 1962), p. 56. See also
   James Joyce, *A Portrait of the Artist as a Young Man* (New York,
   1956), p. 79: Stephen Dedalus 'was conscious of failure and of
   detection, of the squalor of his own mind and home, and felt
   against his neck the raw edge of his turned and jagged collar';
   and D. H. Lawrence, *Lady Chatterley's Lover* (Harmondsworth,
   1973), pp. 148, 226: 'The *care* about money was like a great
   cancer, eating away the individuals of all classes. He [Mellors]
   refused to *care* about money. . . . They are killing off the
   human thing and worshipping the mechanical thing. Money,
   money, money!'
25 George Orwell, 'Not Enough Money' in *Tribune* (London) 327
   (2 April 1943), 15.
26 This is an economic variation of one of D. H. Lawrence's main
   ideas. As Orwell writes in *The Road to Wigan Pier* (Harmondsworth, 1962), p. 146: 'D. H. Lawrence, who was sincere, what-
   ever else he may not have been, expresses the same thought
   over and over again. It is curious how he harps on the idea that
   the English bourgeoisie are all *dead*, or at least gelded.'
27 See Orwell's letter to Eleanor Jacques (1932): 'If we had even
   passable weather, how would it be to go out some Sunday into
   the country, where we could go for a long walk & then have
   lunch at a pub? London is depressing when one has no money'
   (1.107).
28 R. B. Cunninghame Graham, *The Nail-and-Chainmakers: A Plea*.
   London Platform Series, no. 2 (London, 1888), pp. 102–3.
29 Charles Dickens, *Hard Times* (London, 1961), p. 65.
30 *Ibid.*, p. 105.
31 D. H. Lawrence, *Lady Chatterley's Lover*, p. 158.
32 A. J. P. Taylor, *English History, 1914–1945* (New York, 1965), p.
   238.
33 George Orwell, 'Our Own Have Nots' in *Time and Tide*
   XVIII (27 November 1937), 1588.

34 In comparison to Orwell's book, J. B. Priestley's *English Journey* (1934) gives a superficial 'outsider's' view and conveys the impression of a rather cosy and pleasant jaunt.

35 Orwell's desire to change things is related to another criticism of most Left-wing writing. He states in 'England Your England': 'The immediately striking thing about all these papers is their generally negative, querulous attitude, their complete lack at all times of any constructive suggestion' (II.74).

36 *Down and Out*, p. 143.

37 He can also be very muddled-headed about them, as when he projects his *own* feelings about school and writes in *Wigan Pier*, pp. 103–4: 'Of course I know now that there is not one working-class boy in a thousand who does not pine for the day when he will leave school.' In a time of widespread unemployment there would be no economic incentive for leaving school.

38 Victor Brombert, *The Intellectual Hero* (Chicago, 1964), p. 153.

39 *Ibid.*, p. 154.

40 'E' is his wife Eileen, 'G' his sister-in-law Gwen O'Shaughnessy.

41 Victor Gollancz, Preface to *The Road to Wigan Pier* (London, 1937), pp. xvii, xxi, xvi.

42 *Ibid.*, pp. xviii, xx, xxi.

43 See II.431 for the list of atrocities that Orwell compiled.

44 George Orwell, Introduction to *British Pamphleteers*, p. 16.

5 Orwell's Apocalypse: *Coming Up For Air*

1 George Orwell, *Coming Up For Air* (Harmondsworth, 1962), p. 160.

2 George Orwell, *The Road to Wigan Pier* (Harmondsworth, 1962), p. 16.

3 See Orwell's BBC talk (no. 31) 'Calling All Students' (13 June 1943).

4 John Wain, 'Here Lies Lower Binfield' in *Essays on Literature and Ideas* (London, 1963), p. 208.

5 E. M. Forster, 'Abinger Pageant' in *Abinger Harvest* (New York, 1955), p. 343.

6 Isaac Rosenfeld, 'Decency and Death' in *Partisan Review* XVII (May 1950), 516.

7 D. H. Lawrence, 'The Captain's Doll' in *Four Short Novels of D. H. Lawrence* (New York, 1965), p. 245.

8 George Orwell, 'The Male Byronic' in *Tribune* (London), 21 June 1940, p. 20. Orwell's novel has thematic affinities with Wells's *Mr Britling Sees It Through* (1916), which portrays the destruction of these 'golden years' by the Great War.

9 *The Collected Letters of D. H. Lawrence*, ed. Harry Moore, Vol. I (New York, 1962), p. 378 (to Lady Cynthia Asquith, November 1915).

10 Leonard Woolf, *Downhill All the Way* (London, 1967), p. 9.

6 'An Affirming Flame': *Homage to Catalonia*

1 In the same essay Orwell writes: 'To say "I accept" in an age like our own is to say that you accept concentration camps, rubber truncheons, Hitler, Stalin, bombs, aeroplanes, tinned foods, machine guns, putsches, purges, slogans, Bedaux belts, gas masks, submarines, spies, provocateurs, press censorship, secret prisons, aspirins, Hollywood films, and political murders' (I.499–500).

2 Fyodor Dostoyevsky, *The Brothers Karamazov* (New York, 1943), p. 356.

3 John Wain, 'Orwell in Perspective' in *New World Writing* XII (1957), 85.

4 Hugh Thomas, *The Spanish Civil War* (New York, 1963), p. 424n.

5 The first part of Malraux's *Days of Hope* (1938), which combines *reportage*, propaganda and ideology with a fictional account of Malraux's experience of contemporary history, describes the initial events of the war, and the victory of the workers in Madrid and Barcelona.

6 George Orwell, *Homage to Catalonia* (Harmondsworth, 1962), p. 46. Orwell may have been thinking of Pound's *Homage to Sextus Propertius* (1917) and Eliot's *Homage to John Dryden* (1924) when he chose his title.

7 Joseph Conrad, *Nostromo* (New York, 1960), pp. 83, 99.

8 Georges Bernanos, *A Diary of My Times* (New York, 1938), p. 185.

9 By Remarque, Barbusse, Hemingway, Aldington, Graves, Sassoon and Max Plowman.

10 It is interesting to note how images of Burma reappear as similes in *Homage*. The Spanish hills are 'wrinkled like the skins of elephants', a patrol is like 'stalking a wild animal', returning

to Barcelona is like going from Mandalay to a hill station, and the noise of bullets is 'like a tropical rainstorm'.

11 Yet Richard Rees, *George Orwell: Fugitive From the Camp of Victory* (Carbondale, Illinois, 1962), p. 60, writes, 'It is predominantly a gay book.'

12 Quoted in Nathan Cohen, 'A Conversation with Joyce Cary' in *Tamarack Review* III (1957), 15.

13 Compare Orwell's metaphorical and emotional description with Georges Kopp's more precise and factual account in a letter from Barcelona on 31 May 1937:

Eric was wounded on the 20th of May at 5 a.m. The bullet entered the neck just under the larynx, slightly on the left side of its vertical axis, and went out at the dorsal right side of the neck's base. It was a normal 7 mm bore, copper-plated, Spanish Mauser bullet, shot from a distance of some 175 yards. At this range, it has a velocity of some 600 feet per second and a cauterising temperature. Under the impact, Eric fell on his back. The hemorrhaging was insignificant. (British Museum Additional MS 49384.)

14 Orwell's striking change of attitude toward war and politics is similar to T. E. Lawrence's transformation in *Seven Pillars of Wisdom*. In the beginning of the book Lawrence sees the Arabian campaign as a jolly adventure and narrates it in schoolboy terms. But after the capture of Aqaba he realizes the full horror of war, and *Seven Pillars* ends with a massacre and a corrosive description of the Turkish hospital in Damascus, where the rats 'gnawed wet red galleries' through the putrid corpses.

15 The Independent Labour Party was more radical than the Labour Party and, according to A. J. P. Taylor, was 'a refuge for middle-class idealists' (*English History, 1914–1945*, New York, 1965, p. 238).

The differences between the Communist Party and the Independent Labour Party reflected the conflict between Stalin and Trotsky, which Orwell portrayed in *Animal Farm*. Robert Dowse, *Left in the Centre: The Independent Labour Party, 1893–1940* (London, 1966), p. 196, writes: 'From the beginning the CP argued that social revolution in Spain must be secondary to the mobilization of the Spanish people against Franco, whilst the ILP believed that both could be achieved under

Socialist leadership. Policy differences were sharpened by Communist attacks on POUM.'

John McNair was the ILP representative in Barcelona. The CNT were 'Syndicalist unions controlled by the Anarchists'.

16 Thomas, p. 191. See Franz Borkenau, *The Spanish Cockpit* (London, 1937), p. 73, on Barcelona in August 1936:

All languages are spoken and there is an indescribable atmosphere of political enthusiasm, of enjoying the adventure of war, of relief that sordid years of emigration are passed, of absolute confidence in speedy success.

Orwell calls this work 'by a long way the ablest book that has yet appeared on the Spanish war'.

17 See Orwell's 'War Diary' (16 June 1940) for a similar thought: 'If the USA is going to submit to conquest as well, there is nothing for it but to die fighting' (II.349).

18 See Leon Trotsky, *The Revolution Betrayed*, transl. Max Eastman (New York, 1965), p. 290: 'The Soviet bureaucracy succeeds, with its treacherous policy of "people's fronts", in insuring the victory of reaction in Spain and France – the Communist International is doing all it can in that direction.'

There are interesting similarities between *Homage* and Malraux's description in *Man's Estate* (1933) of the betrayal in 1927 of the Shanghai workers by the Communist International in Hankow. Both books convey the heroic spirit of men in war, and affirm man's dignity and grandeur in tragic defeat.

19 Orwell is equally confused about England's motives and writes in 1938: 'The real meaning of British foreign policy in the last two years will not become clear until the war in Spain is over' (I.347).

20 Isaac Deutscher, *Stalin: A Political Biography* (New York, 1960), p. 425.

21 André Malraux, *The Walnut Trees of Altenburg* (London, 1952), p. 119.

22 Robert Graves, *Goodbye to All That* (Harmondsworth, 1961), p. 112, describes a similar episode of military humanism:

I saw a German, perhaps seven hundred yards away, through my telescopic sights. He was taking a bath in the German third line. I disliked the idea of shooting a naked man, so I handed the rifle to the sergeant with me. 'Here, take this. You're a better shot than I am.' He got him; but I had not stayed to watch.

23 George Orwell, *The Road to Wigan Pier* (Harmondsworth, 1962), pp. 132–3.
24 *Ibid.*, p. 130.
25 Malraux describes the same feeling of emotional and political solidarity in the famous descent from the mountain at Teruel, the poignant finale of *Days of Hope*: 'It had begun to drizzle. The last stretchers, the peasants from the mountains, and the last mules were advancing between the vast background of the rocky landscape over which the dark rain-clouds were massing, and the hundreds of peasants standing motionless with raised fists' (Harmondsworth, 1970, p. 440).
26 See Bernanos, p. 118: 'The Spanish tragedy is a charnel-house. All the mistakes by which Europe is bringing about her death, mistakes which she tries to spew forth in frightful convulsions, mingle there in putrefaction.'
27 For a vivid account of Fascist jails, see Arthur Koestler's *Spanish Testament* (1938).
28 Orwell's descriptions of dawn with 'the first narrow streaks of gold, like swords slitting the darkness'; of the cherries whitening on the trees in no man's land; and of the silver poplar leaves that 'fringed our trenches and brushed against my face', are deeply moving affirmations of life. These glimpses suggest the 'real' Spain that Orwell could never see until he was discharged: the goatherds, vineyards, castles and mountains that had held his imagination since childhood.
29 Stephen Spender, *World Within World* (Berkeley, 1966), p. 187.
30 George Orwell, 'Review of *The Forge* by Arturo Barea' in *Horizon* IV (September 1941), 214. See also K. W. Watkins, *Britain Divided: The Effect of the Spanish Civil War on British Public Opinion* (1963).

7 The Political Allegory of *Animal Farm*

1 See Leon Trotsky, *The Revolution Betrayed*, transl. Max Eastman (New York, 1965), pp. 51–2: 'With the utmost stretch of fancy it would be difficult to imagine a contrast more striking than that which exists between the schema of the workers' state

according to Marx, Engels and Lenin, and the actual state now headed by Stalin.'

2 See James Boswell, *Life of Johnson* (London, 1961), p. 1357: Miss Seward told Dr Johnson

'... of a wonderful learned pig, which I had seen at Nottingham; and which did all that we have observed exhibited by dogs and horses.' The subject amused him. 'Then, (said he,) the pigs are a race unjustly calumniated. ... We do not allow *time* for his education.'

3 Jonathan Swift, *Gulliver's Travels and Other Writings* (New York, 1958), p. 224.

4 George Orwell, *Animal Farm* (Harmondsworth, 1970), p. 24.

5 George Orwell, *Coming Up For Air* (Harmondsworth, 1962), pp. 219–20.

6 John Atkins, *George Orwell: A Literary Study* (London, 1954), p. 221.

7 Christopher Hollis, *A Study of George Orwell* (Chicago, 1956), pp. 140, 145, 150.

8 Richard Rees, *George Orwell: Fugitive From the Camp of Victory* (Carbondale, Illinois, 1962), p. 85.

9 Edward Thomas, *Orwell* (London, 1965), p. 71.

10 George Woodcock, *The Crystal Spirit: A Study of George Orwell* (Boston, 1966), p. 192.

11 One line of his speech is borrowed from Hobbes. Compare *Leviathan* (New York, 1962), p. 100: 'The life of man [is] solitary, poor, nasty, brutish, and short' and Major's: 'Our lives are miserable, laborious, and short'.

12 See the last sentence of *The Road to Wigan Pier*: the middle classes 'may sink without further struggles into the working class where we belong, and probably when we get there it will not be so dreadful as we feared, for, after all, we have nothing to lose but our aitches'.

13 See C. M. Bowra, *The Creative Experiment* (New York, 1967), p. 127, on Mayakovsky: 'He became more and more a public figure, a tribune of the Revolution, who through his rhetorical verse did much to convince the proletariat that it lived in a wonderful world and must make every effort to preserve and improve it.' Orwell had read Bowra's essay on Mayakovsky (see III.105).

14 By an anonymous Russian poetaster, quoted in Louis Fischer, *The Life and Death of Stalin* (London, 1953), p. 32.

15 See Robert Tucker and Stephen Cohen (eds.), *The Great Purge Trial* (New York, 1965), p. xviii, quoting Stalin: 'To choose one's victim, to prepare one's plans minutely, to slake an implacable vengeance, and then to go to bed ... there is nothing sweeter in the world.'

16 Isaac Deutscher, *The Prophet Unarmed, Trotsky, 1921–1929* (New York, 1959), p. 28.

17 *Ibid.*, p. 288.

18 Isaac Deutscher, *Stalin: A Political Biography* (New York, 1960), p. 311.

19 See *ibid.*, pp. 309–11.

20 Quoted in Woodcock, p. 196.

21 Deutscher, *Stalin*, p. 325.

22 Deutscher, *The Prophet Unarmed*, p. 5.

23 Tucker and Cohen, p. xxix.

24 *Ibid.*, p. xxiii.

25 Isaac Deutscher, *The Prophet Outcast, Trotsky, 1929–1940* (New York, 1963), p. 360.

26 Quoted in Tucker and Cohen, p. 508.

27 B. T. Oxley, *George Orwell* (London, 1967), p. 81, mentions this striking similarity as well as the parallel to the Kronstadt revolt.

28 Tucker and Cohen, p. xxvii and note.

29 Deutscher, *Stalin*, p. 434.

30 *Ibid.*, pp. 519–20.

31 Isaac Deutscher, '*1984* – the Mysticism of Cruelty' in *Russia in Transition and Other Essays* (New York, 1960), p. 263n.

32 Tom Hopkinson, *George Orwell* (London, 1953), p. 29.

33 Laurence Brander, *George Orwell* (London, 1954), p. 171.

34 Joseph Conrad, *Nostromo* (New York, 1960), pp. 406, 414.

8 The Genesis of *1984*

1 See Irving Howe, 'Orwell: History as Nightmare' in *Politics an the Novel* (New York, 1957), pp. 235–51; Langdon Elsbree, 'The Structured Nightmare of *1984*' in *Twentieth Century Literature* V (1959), 135–51; Toshiko Shibata, 'The Road to Nightmare: an Essay on George Orwell' in *Studies in English Language and Literature* (Kyushu U., Fukuoka) XI (1962), 41–53. Others who make the 'nightmare vision' comparison are: Wyndham Lewis, 'Orwell, or Two and Two Make Four'

in *The Writer and the Absolute* (London, 1952), p. 154; Isaac Deutscher, '*1984* – the Mysticism of Cruelty' in *Russia in Transition and Other Essays* (New York, 1960), p. 252; Philip Rieff, 'George Orwell and the Post-Liberal Imagination' in *Kenyon Review* XVI (1954), 54; Max Lerner, Introduction to Jack London's *The Iron Heel* (New York, 1957), p. vii; Samuel Yorks, 'George Orwell: Seer Over His Shoulder' in *Bucknell Review* IX (1960), 33; Frederick Karl, 'George Orwell: The White Man's Burden' in *A Reader's Guide to the Contemporary English Novel* (London, 1962), p. 164; Edward Thomas, *Orwell* (London, 1965), p. 78; and George Woodcock, *The Crystal Spirit: A Study of George Orwell* (Boston, 1966), pp. 67, 218.

2 Howe, p. 250.

3 The Teheran Conference also gave Orwell the idea of three totalitarian super-states, and he writes that what *1984* 'really meant to do is to discuss the implications of dividing the world up into "Zones of influence"' (IV.460).

   See Isaac Deutscher, *Stalin: A Political Biography* (New York, 1960), p. 514:

   In the months that followed the Teheran Conference, the plans for the division of Europe into zones were becoming more and more explicit. ... Politicians and journalists in the allied countries had discussed a condominium of the three great allied powers, each of whom was to wield paramount influence within its own orbit.

4 Orwell is indebted to his earlier description of a hanging in Burma for the details used in this last work:

   'I have known cases where the doctor was obliged to go beneath the gallows and pull the prisoner's legs to ensure decease. Most disagreeable!' 'Wriggling about, eh? That's bad.' (I.47)

   'It was a good hanging,' said Syme reminiscently. 'I think it spoils it when they tie their feet together. I like to see them kicking.' (*1984*, Harmondsworth, 1973, p. 43)

5 Jonathan Swift, *Gulliver's Travels and Other Writings* (New York, 1958), p. 148.

6 Czeslaw Milosz, *The Captive Mind* (New York, 1953), p. 42.

7 Orwell's concept of Thoughtcrime is not a fantasy of the future, and is similar to Matthew v, 28:

'Whoever looketh on a woman to lust after her hath committed adultery with her already in his heart.'

8 Leon Trotsky, *The Revolution Betrayed*, transl. Max Eastman (New York, 1965), pp. 100, 162.

9 Deutscher, *Stalin*, p. 373.

10 George Orwell, *Down and Out in Paris and London* (Harmondsworth, 1940), p. 104.

11 George Orwell, *Keep the Aspidistra Flying* (Harmondsworth, 1962), p. 95.

12 George Orwell, *The Road to Wigan Pier* (Harmondsworth, 1962), pp. 149, 189.

13 George Orwell, *Coming Up For Air* (Harmondsworth, 1962), p. 149.

14 This sentence was quoted by Orwell in his essay on *Gulliver's Travels*.

15 Jack London, *The Iron Heel* (New York, 1957), p. 150.

16 *Coming Up For Air*, p. 148.

17 George Orwell, 'General de Gaulle' in *Manchester Evening News* (5 May 1944), 2.

18 Swift, *Gulliver's Travels*, p. 68.

19 *The Road to Wigan Pier*, p. 132.

20 *Coming Up For Air*, p. 218.

21 George Orwell, *Animal Farm* (Harmondsworth, 1970), pp. 11, 68.

22 John Wain, 'The Last of George Orwell' in *Twentieth Century* CLV (January 1954), 72.

23 *The Road to Wigan Pier*, p. 45.

24 Fyodor Dostoyevsky, *The Brothers Karamazov* (New York, 1943), pp. 308–9.

25 *Ibid.*, p. 314.

26 Bruno Bettelheim, *The Informed Heart* (Glencoe, Illinois, 1960), pp. 109, 242. See André Malraux, *Antimemoirs* (Harmondsworth, 1970), p. 459: 'The attempt to force human beings to despise themselves . . . is something which seems to me to have to do with the very nature of Nazism. It was aimed at making you lose your soul.'

27 *The Letters of Anton Chekhov*, ed. and transl. Constance Garnett (London, 1920), p. 120.

28 Victor Brombert, *The Intellectual Hero* (Chicago, 1964), p. 137.

29 Harold Rosenberg, *The Tradition of the New* (New York, 1965), p. 270.

Conclusion: Critics on Orwell

1 George Woodcock, 'George Orwell' in *The Writer and Politics* (London, 1948), p. 118.

2 V. S. Pritchett, 'George Orwell' in *New Statesman* XXXIX (28 January 1950), 96.

3 Arthur Koestler, 'A Rebel's Progress to George Orwell's Death' in *The Trail of the Dinosaur* (London, 1955), p. 103.

4 Miriam Gross (ed.), *The World of George Orwell* (London, 1971), p. i.

5 Peter Stansky and William Abrahams, *The Unknown Orwell* (London, 1972), p. xiv.

6 E. M. Forster, 'George Orwell' in *Two Cheers For Democracy* (London, 1951), p. 72.

7 Lionel Trilling, 'George Orwell and the Politics of Truth' in *The Opposing Self* (London, 1955), pp. 151–2.

8 John Wain, 'The Last of George Orwell' in *Twentieth Century* CLV (January 1954), 71.

9 Richard Hoggart, 'George Orwell and *The Road to Wigan Pier*' in *Critical Quarterly* VII (1965), 80.

BIBLIOGRAPHY

American and English editions are cited for those books that were published in both countries.

1 WORKS OF GEORGE ORWELL

Down and Out in Paris and London (London and New York, 1933).
Burmese Days (New York, 1934 and London, 1935).
Introduction to *La Vache enragée* (French translation of *Down and Out*), (Paris, 1935).
A Clergyman's Daughter (London, 1935 and New York, 1936).
Keep the Aspidistra Flying (London, 1936 and New York, 1956).
The Road to Wigan Pier (London, 1937 and New York, 1958).
Homage to Catalonia (London, 1938 and New York, 1952).
Coming Up For Air (London, 1939 and New York, 1950).
'Fascism and Democracy', 'Patriots and Revolutionaries' in *The Betrayal of the Left*, ed. Victor Gollancz (London, 1941).
'Culture and Democracy' in *Victory or Vested Interests?* ed. G. D. H. Cole (London and New York, 1942).
'The Rediscovery of Europe', 'Too Hard on Humanity' in *Talking To India* (London, 1943).
'Imaginary Interviews: George Orwell and Jonathan Swift', 'Bernard Shaw', 'Calling All Students'. Typescripts of BBC Broadcasts (1941–43), nos. 14, 26, 31. Orwell Archive, London University.
Animal Farm (London, 1945 and New York, 1946).

Introduction to *British Pamphleteers* (London, 1948 and New York, 1950).

1984 (London and New York, 1949).

Collected Essays, Journalism and Letters, eds. Sonia Orwell and Ian Angus (London and New York, 1968), 4 vols.

'The Freedom of the Press' in *TLS* (15 September 1972), 1037–9.

II CRITICISM

Alldritt, Keith, *The Making of George Orwell* (London, 1969 and New York, 1970).

Atkins, John, *George Orwell: A Literary Study* (London, 1954 and New York, 1955).

Beadon, Roger, 'With Orwell in Burma' in *Listener* LXXXI (29 May 1969), 755.

Brander, Laurence, *George Orwell* (London and New York, 1954).

Calder, Jenni, *Chronicles of Conscience: A Study of George Orwell and Arthur Koestler* (London and Pittsburgh, 1968).

Connolly, Cyril, *Enemies of Promise* (London, 1938 and Boston, 1939).

Deutscher, Isaac, '*1984* – the Mysticism of Cruelty' in *Russia in Transition and Other Essays* (New York, 1960).

Dunn, Avril, 'My Brother, George Orwell' in *Twentieth Century* CLXIX (March 1961), 255–61.

Fen, Elisaveta, 'George Orwell's First Wife' in *Twentieth Century* CLXVIII (August 1960), 115–26.

Forster, E. M., 'George Orwell' in *Two Cheers For Democracy* (London and New York, 1951).

Fyvel, T. R., 'A Case for George Orwell' in *Twentieth Century* CLX (September 1956), 254–9.

'George Orwell and Eric Blair: Glimpses of a Dual Life' in *Encounter* XIII (July 1959), 60–65.

Gollancz, Victor, Foreword to *The Road to Wigan Pier* (London, 1937).

Green, Martin, 'British Decency' in *Mirror for Anglo-Saxons* (New York, 1960 and London, 1961).

Greenblatt, Stephen, *Three Modern Satirists: Waugh, Orwell and Huxley* (New Haven, Conn., 1965).

Gross, Miriam (ed.), *The World of George Orwell* (London, 1971 and New York, 1972).

Heppenstall, Rayner, *Four Absentees* (London, 1960 and New York, 1962).

Hoggart, Richard, 'George Orwell and *The Road to Wigan Pier*' in *Critical Quarterly* VII (1965), 72–85.

Hollis, Christopher, *A Study of George Orwell* (London and Chicago, 1956).

Hopkinson, Tom, *George Orwell* (British Council pamphlet, London, 1953).

Howe, Irving, 'Orwell: History as Nightmare' in *Politics and the Novel* (New York, 1957).

  (ed.), *Orwell's 'Nineteen Eighty Four': Text, Sources, Criticism* (New York, 1963).

Hynes, Samuel (ed.), *Twentieth Century Interpretations of '1984'* (Englewood Cliffs, N.J., 1971).

Koestler, Arthur, 'A Rebel's Progress to George Orwell's Death' in *The Trail of the Dinosaur* (London and New York, 1955).

Kubal, David, *Outside the Whale: George Orwell's Art and Politics* (Notre Dame, Indiana, 1972).

Lee, Robert, *Orwell's Fiction* (London and Notre Dame, Indiana, 1969).

Lewis, Wyndham, 'Orwell, or Two and Two Make Four' in *The Writer and the Absolute* (London, 1952).

Lief, Ruth Ann, *Homage to Oceania: The Prophetic Vision of George Orwell* (Columbus, Ohio, 1969).

Lutman, Stephen, 'Orwell's Patriotism' in *Journal of Contemporary History* II (1967), 149–58.

Macdonald, Dwight, 'Varieties of Political Experience' in *New Yorker* XXXV (28 March 1959), 137–46.

Mander, John, 'One Step Forward: Two Steps Back' in *The Writer and Commitment* (London, 1961 and Chester Springs, Pa., 1962).

McCarthy, Mary, 'The Writing on the Wall' in *New York Review of Books* (30 January 1969), 3–6.

Meyers, Jeffrey, 'George Orwell' in *Bulletin of Bibliography* XXXI (July–September 1974), 117–21.

    'Review of *The World of George Orwell*, ed. Miriam Gross, and Raymond Williams' *George Orwell*' in *Commonweal* XCVI (2 June 1972), 313–14.

    'Review of Stansky and Abrahams' *The Unknown Orwell*' in *Modern Fiction Studies* XIX (Summer 1973), 250–56.

Modern Fiction Studies XXI (Spring 1975). (Special issue on Orwell.)

Morris, John, ' "Some Are More Equal Than Others": A Note on George Orwell' in *Penguin New Writing* XL (1950), 90–97.

Muggeridge, Malcolm, Introduction to *Burmese Days* (London, 1967).

O'Brien, Conor Cruise, 'Orwell Looks at the World' in *Writers and Politics* (London and New York, 1965).

Oxley, B. T., *George Orwell* (London, 1967 and New York, 1969).

Potts, Paul, 'Don Quixote on a Bicycle: In Memoriam, George Orwell, 1903–1950' in *London Magazine* IV (March 1957), 39–47.

Powell, Anthony, 'George Orwell: A Memoir' in *Atlantic Monthly* CCXX (October 1967), 62–8.

Pritchett, V. S., 'George Orwell' in *Living Writers*, ed. Gilbert Phelps (London, 1947).

    'George Orwell' in *New Statesman* XXXIX (28 January 1950), 96.

Rees, Richard, *George Orwell: Fugitive From the Camp of Victory* (London, 1961 and Carbondale, Illinois, 1962).

Rieff, Philip, 'George Orwell and the Post-Liberal Imagination' in *Kenyon Review* XVI (1954), 49–70.

Rosenfeld, Isaac, 'Decency and Death' in *Partisan Review* XVII (May 1950), 514–18.

Russell, Bertrand, 'Symptoms of Orwell's *1984*' in *Portraits From Memory* (London and New York, 1956).

Spender, Stephen, 'Anti-Vision and Despair' in *The Creative*

Element (London, 1953 and New York, 1954).

Stansky, Peter, and William Abrahams, *The Unknown Orwell* (London and New York, 1972).

Steiner, George, 'True to Life' in *New Yorker* XLV (29 March 1969), 139–51.

Symons, Julian, 'Orwell – A Reminiscence' in *London Magazine* III (September 1963), 35–49.

Thomas, Edward, *Orwell* (London, 1965 and New York, 1968).

Trilling, Lionel, 'George Orwell and the Politics of Truth' in *The Opposing Self* (London and New York, 1955).

Voorhees, Richard, *The Paradox of George Orwell* (Lafayette, Indiana, 1961).

Wain, John, 'Here Lies Lower Binfield' in *Encounter* XVII (October 1961), 70–83.

'The Last of George Orwell' in *Twentieth Century* CLV (January 1954), 71–8.

'Orwell' in *Spectator* 193 (19 November 1954), 630–34.

'Orwell and the Intelligentsia' in *Encounter* XXI (December 1968), 72–80.

'Orwell in Perspective' in *New World Writing* XII (1957), 84–96.

Warburg, Fredric, 'From Wigan to Barcelona' in *An Occupation For Gentlemen* (London, 1959 and New York, 1960).

'Animal Farm' and *'1984'* in *All Authors Are Equal* (London, 1973).

Weintraub, Stanley, 'Homage to Utopia' in *The Last Great Cause: The Intellectuals and the Spanish Civil War* (London and New York, 1968).

West, Anthony, 'George Orwell' in *Principles and Persuasions* (New York, 1957 and London, 1958).

Williams, Raymond, *George Orwell* (London and New York, 1971).

Woodcock, George, *The Crystal Spirit: A Study of George Orwell* (Boston, 1966 and London, 1967).

World Review XVI (June 1950), 3–60. (Special issue on Orwell.)

INDEX